1& 2 CORINTHIANS

Also by Tara-Leigh Cobble

The Bible Recap:
A One-Year Guide to Reading and Understanding the Entire Bible

The Bible Recap Study Guide:
Daily Questions to Deepen Your Understanding of the Entire Bible

The Bible Recap Journal:
Your Daily Companion to the Entire Bible

The Bible Recap Discussion Guide:
Weekly Questions for Group Conversation on the Entire Bible

The Bible Recap Kids' Devotional:
365 Reflections and Activities for Children and Families

The Bible Recap for Kids:
A 365-Day Guide through the Bible for Young Readers

The God Shot:
100 Snapshots of God's Character in Scripture

Israel: Beauty, Light, and Luxury

The Bible Recap Knowing Jesus Series*

Knowing Jesus as King:
A 10-Session Study on the Gospel of Matthew

Knowing Jesus as Servant:
A 10-Session Study on the Gospel of Mark

Knowing Jesus as Savior:
A 10-Session Study on the Gospel of Luke

Knowing Jesus as God:
A 10-Session Study on the Gospel of John

The Bible Recap Knowing God Series*

Acts: The Spirit and the Bride—a
10-Week Bible Study on God and His Church

Romans: Dead to Sin and Alive to Christ—
a 10-Week Bible Study

* General editor

THE BIBLE RECAP KNOWING GOD SERIES

1 & 2 CORINTHIANS

LOVE, UNITY, AND THE COUNTER-CULTURAL POWER OF THE CROSS

A 10-WEEK BIBLE STUDY

TARA-LEIGH COBBLE,

GENERAL EDITOR

WRITTEN BY THE D-GROUP THEOLOGY & CURRICULUM TEAM

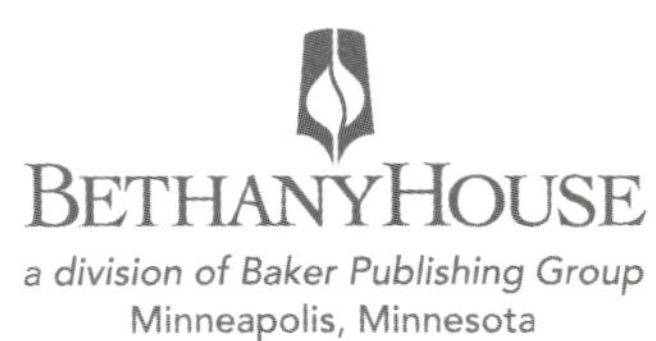

a division of Baker Publishing Group
Minneapolis, Minnesota

Published by Bethany House Publishers
Minneapolis, Minnesota
BethanyHouse.com

Bethany House Publishers is a division of
Baker Publishing Group, Grand Rapids, Michigan

Printed in the United States of America

Library of Congress Cataloging-in-Publication Data
Names: Cobble, Tara-Leigh, author.
Title: 1 & 2 Corinthians : love, unity, and the countercultural power of the cross : a 10 week Bible study / Tara-Leigh Cobble.
Other titles: 1 and 2 Corinthians
Description: Minneapolis, Minnesota : Bethany House Publishers, a division of Baker Publishing Group, [2025] | Series: The Bible recap knowing God series | Includes bibliographical references.
Identifiers: LCCN 2025001601 | ISBN 9780764243622 (paperback) | ISBN 9781493446933 (ebook)
Subjects: LCSH: Bible. Corinthians—Commentaries. | Bible. Corinthians—Study and teaching. | Jesus Christ—Crucifixion—Biblical teaching.
Classification: LCC BS2675.53 .C63 2025 | DDC 227/.2—dc23/eng/20250215
LC record available at https://lccn.loc.gov/2025001601

The D-Group Theology & Curriculum Team is Laura Buchelt, Emily Pickell, Abbey Dane, Kirsten McCloskey, Emma Dotter, Liz Suggs, and Tara-Leigh Cobble.

The general editor is represented by Alive Literary Agency, AliveLiterary.com.

Cover design by Dan Pitts

Baker Publishing Group publications use paper produced from sustainable forestry practices and postconsumer waste whenever possible.

25 26 27 28 29 30 31 7 6 5 4 3 2 1

CONTENTS

INTRODUCTION TO 1 CORINTHIANS

The apostle Paul wrote thirteen of the New Testament's twenty-seven books, but when they were penned, they weren't in book form at all. You might have heard Paul's writings referred to as the "Pauline Epistles," which is just a formal way of saying that these books were Paul's letters. It's important to keep in mind that each of his letters was written at a specific time to a specific group of people. In other words, these letters weren't written *to* us today, but they've been preserved *for* us in Scripture and still hold value in our lives as Christ-followers.

With that in mind, let's lay out some ground rules for our study. Context is vital to understanding Scripture, and understanding Scripture is vital to applying it. If you come across something that seems like a concrete command or truth from Paul, cross-reference it with other letters in the New Testament. If it doesn't come up elsewhere, there's a good chance it was written in response to a specific event or circumstance his original audience was experiencing. When that happens, instead of zooming in, try zooming out to find the overarching principle. We never want to build entire doctrines on a single verse without understanding the context.

Scholars strongly believe Paul may have written at least four letters to the Corinthians; however, only two of these letters have been found. His first was likely sent prior to 1 Corinthians, so for the sake of clarity in this study, we'll call that letter 0 Corinthians. And the other was likely written between 1 and 2 Corinthians, so we'll refer to that as 1.5 Corinthians.

Paul wrote 1 Corinthians while he was in Ephesus, roughly between AD 55 and 57 (Acts 18). At the time, Greece was divided into two Roman provinces. The northern province was called Macedonia, and the southern province was called Achaia—and that's where Corinth was located. Its location was significant because it was on a major trade route, and it served as host to the Isthmian Games (second in popularity to the Olympics). But Corinth was also the site of the temple to Aphrodite and home to about one thousand "priestesses." Those priestesses were actually temple prostitutes, and that concept paints a pretty compelling picture of the cesspool of sin that made up the debased Greek culture in Corinth.

Here, in this destination-metropolis filled with pagan worship, Paul helped plant the Corinthian church. He knew the believers there well and considered himself their spiritual father. Early in the letter, you'll see evidence that he considered the people of the Corinthian church to be true Christians; he didn't address issues of salvation, but of sanctification (God's work of making Christians holy and more like Jesus). He didn't tell them how to be saved from their sins; rather, he addressed issues of maturity and discipleship (or lack thereof). The Corinthians seemed to think they'd outgrown Paul's teaching and were proud of the "spiritual knowledge" they'd accumulated.

Because the perverse Corinthian culture had permeated the culture of the church, Paul used rhetoric they would understand as he worked to convince them that they'd gotten off track. He sometimes even carried both sides of the conversation, as though responding to the questions he assumed they'd have. Throughout the letter, he changed his tone as needed. At times he peppered his readers with sarcasm and rhetorical questions. He often repeated himself to drive home his points.

It's important to recognize that each letter to the Corinthians is distinct, because different relational dynamics are at play. In 1 Corinthians, Paul wrote to answer some of their questions and to give them sharp, direct guidance on specific issues. He wasn't trying to be mean to them; being the spiritual father that he was, Paul wanted to see repentance from a church that was walking down dangerous paths. By the time he wrote 2 Corinthians, he had seen a lot of growth in their church, and he wanted to encourage more growth and repair their strained relationship.

As you begin studying this first letter (which was probably Paul's second letter to the church in Corinth), remember that Paul loved the Corinthian Christians deeply, even though it may seem like he comes out swinging. Let's jump in!

HOW TO USE THIS STUDY

While Bible study is vital to the Christian walk, a well-rounded spiritual life comes from engaging with other spiritual disciplines as well. This study is designed not only to equip you with greater knowledge and theological depth, but to help you engage in other formative practices that will create a fuller, more fulfilling relationship with Jesus. We want to see you thrive in every area of your life with God!

Content and Questions

In each of the ten weeks of this study, the teaching and questions are divided into six days, but feel free to do it all at once if that's more manageable for your schedule. If you choose to complete each week's study in one sitting (especially if that time occurs later in the study-week), keep in mind that there are aspects you will want to be mindful of each day: the daily Bible reading, Scripture memorization, and the weekly challenge. Those are best attended to throughout the week.

Daily Bible Reading

The daily Bible reading corresponds to our study. It will take an average of three minutes per day to simply read (not study) the text. If you're an auditory learner, you may prefer to listen to an audio version of these Bible chapters.

Even if you decide to do the week's content and questions in one sitting, we still encourage you to make the daily Bible reading a part of your regular daily rhythm. Establishing a habit of reading the Word every day will help fortify your faith and create greater connection with God.

If you decide to break the study up into the six allotted days each week, your daily Bible reading will align with your study. Days 1–5 will follow our study of 1 and 2 Corinthians, Day 6 features a psalm that corresponds to our reading, and Day 7 serves as a catch-up day in case you fall behind.

Scripture Memorization

Memorizing Scripture isn't busywork! It's an important part of hiding God's Word in our hearts (Psalm 119:11). Our memorization passage—1 Corinthians 13:1–13—focuses on God's perfect love and what it looks like to live as His beloved, revealing His love to the world around us. We encourage you to practice it cumulatively—that is, *add* to what you're practicing each week instead of *replacing* it. We quote the English Standard Version (and some of our resources are in that translation as well), but feel free to memorize it in whatever translation you prefer. We suggest working on each week's verse(s) throughout the week, not just at the last minute. We've provided some free tools to help you with this, including a weekly verse song: MyDGroup.org/Resources/Corinthians.

Weekly Challenge

This is our practical response to what we've learned each week. We want to be "doers of the word, and not hearers only" (James 1:22). You'll find a variety of challenges, and we encourage you to lean into them all—especially the ones you find *most* challenging! This will help strengthen your spiritual muscles and encourage you in your faith. As with the memory verse, you'll want to begin this practice earlier in the week, especially because some weekly challenges include things to do each day of the week (e.g., prayers, journaling, etc.).

Resources

This is a Scripture-heavy study, and you'll find yourself looking up passages often. If you're new to studying Scripture, this will be a great way to dig in and sharpen your skills! You will feel more equipped and less intimidated as you move through each chapter. Some questions may ask you to refer to a Bible dictionary, commentary, or Greek or Hebrew lexicon, but you don't need to purchase those tools. There are lots of free options available online. We've linked to some of our favorite tools—plus additional resources such as podcasts, articles, and apps—at MyDGroup.org/Resources/Corinthians.

Groups

Because each week has a lot of questions in the content, we offer the following recommendation for those who plan to discuss the study in a weekly group meeting. As each member is doing their homework, we suggest they mark their favorite items with a star and mark any confusing items with a question mark. This serves as preparation for the group discussion and helps direct the conversation in beneficial ways. Group leaders, please note the starred prompts in each chapter; we've highlighted these for you as topics you may find helpful to prioritize in group discussions.

WEEK 1

1 Corinthians 1–3

Scripture to Memorize

If I speak in the tongues of men and of angels, but have not love, I am a noisy gong or a clanging cymbal.

1 Corinthians 13:1

Note: If you haven't yet read How to Use This Study on pages 9–11, please do that before continuing. It will provide you with a proper framework and helpful tools.

DAILY BIBLE READING

Day 1: 1 Corinthians 1:1–9

Day 2: 1 Corinthians 1:10–17

Day 3: 1 Corinthians 1:18–31

Day 4: 1 Corinthians 2:1–16

Day 5: 1 Corinthians 3:1–23

Day 6: Psalm 1

Day 7: Catch-Up Day

Corresponds to Day 333 of *The Bible Recap*.

WEEKLY CHALLENGE

See page 36 for more information.

DAY 1

1 Corinthians 1:1–9

READ 1 CORINTHIANS 1:1–9

Review 1:1–3.

Right away, Paul established himself as the writer of this letter to the church in Corinth, mentioning Sosthenes, who was likely either a scribe or cowriter. Paul also called himself an apostle. This title carried significant weight for the church at large, and it became an important qualifier for the words Paul had for the church at Corinth.

1. **Look up the word *apostle* in a Bible dictionary and note why this title was important for the believers reading this letter.**

2. According to 1:1, how was Paul given this assignment?

It's not uncommon to think the word *apostle* is synonymous with *disciple*. But the distinction is that apostles were specifically chosen by Jesus to carry the message of the gospel. After Jesus's resurrection and ascension, others were appointed as apostles if they met certain requirements, namely, that they were eyewitnesses to Jesus's life and teaching. Some were also appointed by other apostles. Here, Paul clarified that he was not appointed as an apostle by any man, but that this was a divine appointment by Jesus.

This title was crucial because an apostle carried the authority to speak on Jesus's behalf. For the church at Corinth, it was important that they heard Paul's words through that filter.

3. According to 1:2, what were three ways Paul addressed the recipients of his letter?

Make no mistake—this letter was to a group of believers.

4. What language do you see in 1:2 that promotes unity among the church's members?

Because you've read the introduction (right?), you know the moral "state of the union" in Corinth. Whatever your view of the pagan and promiscuous habits of this city, bring it even lower. Then as we read this letter, remember the word Paul used to describe its recipients: These were *saints*. Despite the cesspool of their surroundings, these were believers whose true identity was in Christ, and Paul encouraged them to remain a light in a dark place. They would do that by staying unified in Christ.

★ 5. In what ways have you seen the culture around you influence your own life, habits, and even faith?*

Paul also began this letter by extending grace and peace to his readers—not from himself but "from God our Father and the Lord Jesus Christ."

Despite all we'll discover about the problems that plagued the church at Corinth, their eternal identity was secure in the grace and peace of the Lord Jesus Christ.

Review 1:4–7.

6. Notice throughout this section who "does the doing." Fill in the table below with who was the doer, who was the recipient, and what was done.

Verse	Doer	Recipient	What Was Done
1:4	Christ Jesus	The church	Grace of God was given
1:5			
1:6			
1:7			

Paul began this section by giving thanks to God for all that was going well among the believers in Corinth. Paul, in a spirit of gratitude, peace, and love for the saints, had some words of correction for them as his letter continued. But those words didn't negate all the positive work and forward progress this church had experienced.

* Starred prompts are specifically designed to be useful for group discussion.

★ 7. Are you ever tempted to negate the work Christ has done in your life when you feel you've failed in a particular area? How might this blind you to the ways God is growing you?

Review 1:8–9.

No matter what the believers in Corinth faced—no matter the temptation they might've experienced or even the ways they might've fallen—Paul assured them they would be guiltless in the day of Jesus's return. Why? *Because God is faithful.*

Paul's confidence was not in the Corinthians' behavior. It was in the faithfulness of God. They were called into the fellowship of Christ the same way he was—by the will of God. And what God initiates, He will sustain and He will fulfill.

8. How many times is Jesus referred to (by name or by pronoun) in these first nine verses of 1 Corinthians?

Our identity as saints begins and ends with the Lord Jesus Christ. He is the one who sustains us to the end.

DAY 2

1 Corinthians 1:10–17

READ 1 CORINTHIANS 1:10–17

Paul's repetition of a word from yesterday's reading (*brothers*) sets us up well for the rebuke in today's section. What may feel like an abrupt change in tone from his gracious and peaceful greeting was actually a call to lean into their true identity and union in Christ.

1. Look back at 1:9 and fill in the blank: "God is faithful, by whom you were called into the ________________ of his Son, Jesus Christ our Lord."

The translation of the Greek word used here is *koinōnia*, and its synonyms include *community*, *communion*, and *joint participation*.[1] Unfortunately, these were not terms that described the experience of the Corinthian church.

Review 1:10.

Here, Paul switched to a point of correction toward the church, but he did it with the same voice of love we saw in the first nine verses. He didn't simply ask them to stop being divided. He was imploring them, as the original wording more strongly suggests, to stop *ripping each other apart*.[2]

There wasn't violence happening within the church, but division between church members was damaging and even counter to what it means to be united with Christ. From Paul's perspective, it felt like the church was being ripped apart from within.

★ 2. Read Psalm 55:12–14. How does strife with a friend or fellow believer carry heavier pain? Can you relate? If so, briefly describe.

Providing a contrast to this word picture of being ripped apart, Paul pleaded with the believers to be united with one another—to be repaired or mended—that they might be one.

3. Read John 17:20–23. What did Jesus pray for all believers everywhere?

Review 1:11–13.

Paul went on to give examples of the report he had received. This is the only mention of Chloe in Scripture. Paul wrote this letter from Ephesus (another city where he helped establish a church), so most scholars believe that Chloe, likely a believer, had business dealings in both Ephesus and Corinth that would allow her to receive reports from those working for her.

4. According to 1:11–12, what did Chloe's people report about the church in Corinth?

This word *follow* in 1:12 suggests allegiance or lordship. The divisions within the church were about the who's who among the preachers.

5. In the table below, write one noteworthy thing you know about each person mentioned in 1:12. Use a commentary for help.

Name	What He's Known For
Paul	
Apollos	
Cephas (Peter)	
Christ	

★ 6. Read Ephesians 4:11–13. Why was the church given apostles, prophets, evangelists, shepherds, and teachers? How had the Corinthians distorted these God-given roles?

The problem wasn't that there were multiple teachers. The problem was that the church was elevating the teacher above the mission. They were boasting about who followed who, when only one person should be their Lord. When Paul referred to Jesus in 1 Corinthians 1, he called Him "the Lord Jesus Christ" or "Jesus Christ our Lord" six times. Paul's allegiance was to Christ alone.

Review 1:14–17.

Paul's reference to his involvement in the church's baptisms was almost comical. He seemed flustered at the notion that there would be any discussion at all over whether he was the one baptizing. Who did the baptizing was never the point. The Corinthians were stuck on this secondary issue and allowed it to diminish the message baptism proclaims.

It seems they were interested in listening to and following whomever they thought was the most compelling speaker. But the gospel doesn't need to be dressed up by anyone. The message of Christ can be just as powerful and life-changing when shared in simple words by unlearned disciples.

DAY 3

1 Corinthians 1:18–31

READ 1 CORINTHIANS 1:18–31

In 1:17, Paul said we don't need eloquent words of wisdom—or as some translations say, "clever speech" (NLT)—when sharing the gospel. Why? Because the power is in the message of the cross.

Review 1:18–22.

Paul shined a floodlight on the contrast between how those who "are perishing" and those who "are being saved" view the cross. These verb tenses are present progressive, meaning they point to a current, ongoing action.

Those who view the cross as foolishness or folly are actively moving away from life and toward death. But for those who believe the cross is the power of God, this power is progressively shaping them into the image of Christ, as a part of their eternal life with Him. There is no in-between; everyone is either actively perishing or actively being saved.

★ 1. Describe the hope this gives you as a believer to know that nothing can stop God's work of salvation in your life. How does this create urgency to share the message of Jesus with the lost?

When you stop to ponder the message of the cross—the pure logistics of it all—it may sound outlandish. Yet belief in this astonishing but true message is the path to God's freedom in our lives.

2. In 1:20, Paul demanded an answer from three groups of people. Who were they?

At that time and in that place, acquiring more knowledge was the name of the game. Names such as Aristotle, Socrates, and Plato were part of their heritage, and the Greeks took great pride in the "wisdom" they acquired through debates and lectures from celebrity orators. The Greeks highly valued wisdom but looked for it in the wrong places.

This is not that different from our modern culture. We have more information available to us than ever, and worldly wisdom questions the message of the cross—mocks it, even.

3. In 1:21, how did God use the "folly" of what Paul and his fellow missionaries taught?

The world may think the gospel is preposterous. But that doesn't make it less true—and it doesn't diminish its power.

Review 1:23–25.

4. Fill in the blanks in 1:23 below.

"We preach ______________ ______________________."

The Jews understood the meaning of "Christ"—their anticipated Messiah. Living under the tyrannical rule of the occupying Romans, the Jews were waiting for the Christ and His cavalry to come set them free from earthly oppression. So Christ *crucified*? It made no sense to them. And the Greeks, with their history of powerful, knowledgeable leaders, couldn't concede to the idea of a king wearing a crown of thorns.

★ 5. What do you think Paul meant by "the foolishness of God" and "the weakness of God" in 1:25? Use a commentary for help.

Review 1:26–31.

Modern Christians put a lot of stock into figuring out our "calling." Many spend years trying to figure out what they are "called to do with their lives." But our calling is not about our "doing" at all. It's surrendering our lives to God's wisdom and direction. He will do the rest.

6. In 1:27–28, what phrase appears three times?

In God's upside-down kingdom, the people who were considered foolish—those in whom society saw no value—were the ones chosen by God to carry the message of the cross.

Do you often find yourself feeling like you don't belong in the kingdom? Maybe you feel you don't have as much knowledge as other believers. Maybe your past (or present) is littered with mistakes and missteps. Maybe you feel like the weak link in God's plan for redemption. If any of that feels familiar, let the warmth of 1:30 wash over you.

7. Fill in the blanks.

"And ______________ ____ ______, you are ____ ___________ ________,

who became to us wisdom from God, ________________________ and

________________________ and __________________."

Because of Christ crucified, you *were made* righteous (made clean before God, once and for all). Because of Christ crucified, you *are being* sanctified (continually made more and more into the likeness of Jesus). Because of Christ crucified, you *will be* redeemed (set free forever). What 1:30 assures us is that "Christ crucified" means we are being saved—and He does the doing.

Now, that doesn't sound so foolish.

DAY 4

1 Corinthians 2:1–16

 **READ 1 CORINTHIANS 2:1–16**

Review 2:1–5.

When Paul visited the church in Corinth, he made a decision about how he would relate to them; he decided he would know nothing—except Christ crucified. He could have come "with lofty speech or wisdom" (2:1), but he chose to take a simpler approach in presenting the gospel to them.

1. Based on Philippians 3:4–6, how was Paul's approach counterintuitive to his Hebrew pedigree?

Though Paul could have gone toe-to-toe with any of the great speakers and teachers of the day, he set all of that aside to let the power of the gospel have the spotlight. He humbled himself when he could've proven himself. He even made himself vulnerable by sharing with them the "weakness, fear, and much trembling" (see 2:3) he wrestled with while he was previously in Corinth.

2. Read Acts 18:9–11. What helped Paul overcome his fear and stay in Corinth?

Paul could have relied on his wealth of knowledge to help him during that time, but that would have been to the eternal detriment of the lost people in the city.

3. In 1 Corinthians 2:4–5, what did Paul rely on as he spoke to the Corinthians? What was the purpose of that?

Review 2:6–9.

In 2:6, Paul clarified that it was important to share wisdom and knowledge, even with the mature believer—we are all ever-growing in our knowledge of Christ. However, he stressed the importance of growing in this "hidden wisdom" of God—not the wisdom of this age that is passing away.

It might seem strange that the secret and wisdom of God would be for our glory, because the believer's purpose in life includes glorifying God and making Him known. And certainly we should beware of anyone who uses this passage to justify self-glorification. But as we mature as image bearers of God, we'll look more and more like Christ—transformed into His likeness "from one degree of glory to another" (2 Corinthians 3:18).

In 2:8, Paul expressed how much stock he put into the wisdom of the rulers of this age—they were the ones who were so blind to the truth that they crucified "the Lord of glory." Clearly, their wisdom could not be trusted.

Paul quoted the prophet Isaiah in 2:9; and while we may assume this referred to a future glory when we are with Christ, the context of the passage shows that God gives special revelations to the spiritual man through the Holy Spirit. No natural man can even conceive of what is available to the believer through the riches of Christ.

Review 2:10–13.

4. The Spirit (capital *S*) is mentioned five times here. List every function of the Spirit in these verses.

5. In John 16:13, what did Jesus say the Spirit will do for the believer?

Because we are believers, we can view the world through a spiritual lens. We can receive guidance by the Spirit, receive instruction by the Spirit, and be given insight by the Spirit.

★ 6. Have you ever sensed instruction from the Holy Spirit to take a step of obedience? Briefly describe one memorable instance.

Review 2:14–16.

Essentially, Paul said the natural, or unsaved, person is the antithesis of the spiritual person. This insight and revelation are not available to them. They can make good decisions and live moral lives, but the guidance of the Lord is not and cannot be revealed to them.

★ 7. Have you ever listened to instruction or advice from an unbeliever instead of seeking the Lord's wisdom? What was the result?

In 2:15, Paul certainly wasn't saying that believers can't be judged (evaluated, questioned, examined)—but rather that believers can, and should, be held accountable only by those with the mind of Christ (believers). Even this, when done correctly, can help fellow believers grow in maturity and godly wisdom, which glorifies Christ.

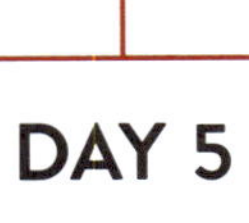

DAY 5

1 Corinthians 3:1–23

READ 1 CORINTHIANS 3:1–23

Review 3:1–4.

1. What two phrases in 3:1 indicate Paul was talking to believers?

Paul turned his attention from the natural man and the spiritual man to the fleshly or carnal Christian—the one who belongs to Christ but acts more like the world. The Corinthians had likely become lax and assumed they were behaving as spiritual people. Paul was essentially saying, *"Not so fast, my friends."*

It may sound insulting for Paul to refer to them as children who needed to be bottle-fed, but this was their reality. It was nearly impossible for the Corinthians to grow in spiritual maturity because they weren't growing in the way God had already instructed them: to be unified.

2. According to 3:3, what two behaviors indicated they were acting in a fleshly way?

Paul drew their attention back to 1:12 and these factions and cliques associated with different leaders. As we'll see later in this letter, the Corinthians weren't entirely unspiritual. In fact, they were blessed with a number of spiritual gifts that served the church well. But Paul addressed this problem of division early on because it threatened to tear the church apart.

3. According to James 3:16, what two things coincide with jealousy and selfish ambition?

Review 3:5–9.

Paul humbly leveled the playing field. He was perhaps one of the most brilliant minds of the day, and Apollos was already a renowned speaker and preacher. But Paul wanted the Corinthians to know that this was merely their function in the body as fellow servants of Christ.

Living in an agrarian culture, the Corinthians certainly would have understood Paul's illustration. Paul, Apollos, and every other believer was entirely dependent on the Spirit to bring the fruits of their labor.

The Corinthian Christians had become oblivious to this truth and elevated their personal preferences over the movement of the Spirit. When we act according to the flesh, we actually tear the church down rather than build it up.

4. Ask God to examine your heart. Do you have a critical spirit about secondary issues or opinions in your church? Is there a complaint or a point of pride that you've elevated above the mission of Christ?

Review 3:10–15.

Switching to an architectural metaphor, Paul compared the collective body of believers to the construction of a building. In any construction project, the foundation is the most crucial part.

5. Paul was a participant in laying the foundation, but according to 3:11, who was the actual foundation of the church? Why is it important that the work be done with care and reverence?

Serving Christ and His kingdom is sacred work. There will come a time, "the Day" (3:13), when all of that work, or our carelessness in it, will be revealed: Is the work lasting? Or temporary? To be clear, the work itself does not determine our salvation, but it will determine whether we receive rewards in the kingdom.

Building the church is also sacred work. And when we do it foolishly or selfishly, the result is destruction, not fruitful building. The church is the place where God Himself dwells among a group of believers. Division, which leads to destruction, is something God takes *very* seriously.

Review 3:16–23.

In case they missed it the first time, Paul reminded the Corinthians of the senselessness of worldly "wisdom" and elevating any man over Christ. There was no reason to boast in worldly things or worldly wisdom because, as believers, we've been given everything in Christ!

In at least five instances leading up to this point, Paul reminded the Corinthians of the gospel (1:8, 18, 30; 2:2; 3:23) and the rock-solid foundation they had in Jesus Christ. Why? Because the only cure for the carnal Christian is to be reminded of the gospel. Forgetting our position in Christ, divisions, and sinful habits can lead to drifting away, but in all of these cases, the gospel can reorient the heart. When we take our eyes off ourselves and focus on Jesus, we begin to grow again as we remember the truth: He's where the joy is!

6. What stood out to you most in this week's study? Why?

7. What did you learn or relearn about God and His character this week?

DAY 6

Corresponding Psalm & Prayer

1. What correlation do you see between Psalm 1 and this week's study?

2. What portions of this psalm stand out to you most?

3. Close by praying this prayer aloud:

Father,

You always do the doing: You made us and You made us righteous. You saved us and You are sanctifying us. You redeemed us and one day You will redeem us forever. Just like You did for the Corinthian church, You made us saints.

And yet, I'm also a sinner. I've been jealous and I've caused strife. I've made much of myself and little of You. I've sown division when You've required unity. I repent.

Lord, let me never walk in the counsel of the wicked. Help me to delight in Your wisdom. Plant me like a tree by Your streams, and let the fruit I bear bring unity to Your church. Like Your Son prayed, make us one.

My allegiance is to You only, so I surrender my life to You, Lord—every moment of my day, each decision I make, I yield my will and way to Your perfect will and way.

I love You too. Amen.

DAY 7

Rest, Catch Up, or Dig Deeper

WEEKLY CHALLENGE

Paul opened 1 Corinthians by celebrating the works God had done in the church. Even though there were issues within their church, those issues didn't negate God's work. It's not uncommon to focus on only our failures before Christ, diminishing the ways He has grown us. Write down at least three ways you've drawn closer to Christ since you came to know Him. Celebrate what He has done in your life!

WEEK 2

1 Corinthians 4–6

Scripture to Memorize

And if I have prophetic powers, and understand all mysteries and all knowledge, and if I have all faith, so as to remove mountains, but have not love, I am nothing.

1 Corinthians 13:2

DAILY BIBLE READING

Day 1: 1 Corinthians 4:1–13

Day 2: 1 Corinthians 4:14–21

Day 3: 1 Corinthians 5:1–13

Day 4: 1 Corinthians 6:1–11

Day 5: 1 Corinthians 6:12–20

Day 6: Psalm 7

Day 7: Catch-Up Day

Corresponds to Days 333 and 334 of *The Bible Recap*.

WEEKLY CHALLENGE

See page 57 for more information.

DAY 1

1 Corinthians 4:1–13

Review 4:1–4.

In our reading so far, Paul warned his readers twice not to put the apostles on a pedestal. So how *should* the Corinthians view the apostles? Paul's answer was simple: Not too low and not too high. The apostles were both servants and stewards.

1. **Look up the word *servants* (4:1) in a Greek lexicon and write the definition below.**

The word used for *servants* was commonly associated with the lowly workers of no social status who rowed in the underbelly (lowest level) of a ship. In contrast, a steward was uniquely selected and *entrusted* to oversee his master's business or property. Through this comparison, Paul communicated that while the apostles were lowly and undeserving, they were also selected by God to pursue His goals and objectives.

Paul was to steward the mysteries of God as he oversaw the churches. These "mysteries" are simply the truths of the Christian faith concerning God's wisdom and the gospel (which can be fully understood only through the Spirit's revelation). For believers, the truth of the gospel and the wisdom of God are no longer mysteries; but the mystery remains for the unbeliever.

Greek culture valued society's elite, and as a "servant," Paul didn't fit their mold. He knew whatever God thought of him was what mattered. He didn't get stuck in a spiral of negative self-talk considering the Corinthians' judgment of (or displeasure with) him. He knew his standing before God was based on his faith in Christ, not on his performance or status.

★ 2. Describe a time when you let others' critique or expectation of your walk with the Lord discourage you. Considering what you've learned from Paul's example, how would you respond differently now?

Review 4:5.

The Corinthians thought they were qualified to make judgment calls about whether Paul was a legitimate apostle. Interestingly, Paul's issue wasn't with the judging. Paul was concerned with the Corinthians' self-promotion prompting the judging. It's like he was saying, "*Who made you in charge? You promoted yourselves.*" This self-promotion evidenced a deeper problem in the hearts of the Corinthians. Their judgments were simply a symptom of their greater sickness.

3. Fill in the blanks in 4:5 below.

"Therefore do not pronounce ______________ before the time, before the Lord comes, who will bring to __________ the things now ____________ in ______________ and will disclose the ______________ of the heart."

Review 4:6–7.

The conclusions the Corinthians drew were incorrect, because the standard they applied was incorrect. The Greeks believed humility was associated with the lowest in society (e.g., slaves) and was a sign of weakness, and this belief had crept into the church.

Paul explained that if the Corinthians had used a biblical standard (i.e., if they'd aligned their preferences with God's), they wouldn't have favored false teachers and they would've protected themselves from the pride that had "puffed them up." As we'll see repeatedly, pride was the disease infecting their hearts.

Review 4:8.

Irony and sarcasm were popular and preferred in Greek rhetoric. Paul wasn't being rude; he was speaking their language. By suggesting the Corinthians had "become kings," Paul revealed their incorrect thinking. Because they'd been evangelized by prominent teachers (not humble apostles), they lived as if they'd already stood before Christ and were reigning and judging the world with Him.

Review 4:9–13.

4. **Using a dictionary, define *exhibited*.**

Paul recalled a parade of a conquering Roman general—where armies, loot, and captives would've been paraded as a spectacle through town. The apostles were a spectacle, because they'd been publicly humiliated for the sake of Christ. But by including the angels as spectators, Paul clarified that the spiritual realm was watching too.

Everything Paul did—especially earning his own living—was a cultural disgrace, but Paul responded to his critics as Jesus would have. Though the apostles were treated like dust swept up in a dustpan and thrown into the trash, Paul chose to live with a kingdom mindset: A humble, godly lifestyle is always the best choice for believers.

DAY 2

1 Corinthians 4:14–21

 **READ 1 CORINTHIANS 4:14–21**

Review 4:14–15.

The harshness of Paul's communication style matched the gravity of the Corinthians' sin (pride). By using the metaphor of a father and child, Paul reminded the church of his love and intention: He wanted to help them look like Jesus. A proper response to his message would have been for them to repent and imitate his humility.

1. **Using a Bible dictionary, fill in the table below.**

Word	Definition
Shame	
Humility	
Discipleship	

The Greek word for "guides" often referred to a servant responsible for babysitting his master's young boy. There was a key difference between the assigned guide and the father: The guide could be replaced. Paul was the father in the metaphor due to his active role in founding the Corinthian church. He'd been consistently involved.

Because Paul was an apostle, he held unique spiritual authority over the whole church. His instruction impacted the entire congregation. Leading an individual (or group of individuals) to Christ doesn't give you authority over them; yet it typically should lead to an influential relationship: discipleship (Matthew 28:19–20).

★ 2. Paul used sarcasm to correct the Corinthians, and it was culturally appropriate. How might you correct someone you're discipling without shaming them for missing the mark?

Review 4:16–17.

While it seems simple, Paul's call for the Corinthians to mirror his way of life was radical. He didn't want the Corinthians to look like his biggest fans—he wanted them to look like Jesus. (Remember, there weren't Bibles he could hand out, so imitation was a key component of both discipleship and apostolic leadership.) Imitation demands presence, so Paul sent Timothy to visit the Corinthians.

Review 4:18–19.

Some of the believers in Corinth were arrogant and thought Paul was afraid to visit. Others flat-out didn't respect him, so they acted as if they'd never see him again. The only problem was, Paul planned to show up.

3. Write 4:19 below and circle the phrase that adds a caveat to Paul's commitment to visit.

Some of the Corinthians weren't taking Paul seriously, but he knew the truth would be revealed when he visited them. He wanted to visit them, but he'd only be able to accomplish that visit if God, in His sovereignty, made a way for it to happen. And his visit wasn't motivated by the pride of proving himself right; instead, he was committed to being faithful to God's leading and timing.

Review 4:20–21.

The phrase "kingdom of God" refers to the reign of the eternal and all-powerful God of the universe. More specifically, "the kingdom of God" can refer to those within the kingdom who've committed to submit to God's rule and God's way.

4. **Do a quick internet search.** How many times did Jesus reference the kingdom of God?

The kingdom of God was the most common topic in Jesus's teaching, and it was regularly paired with a reference to divine power—life in the kingdom isn't marked simply by a way of speaking or thinking. Paul knew this all too well: Those in the kingdom are marked by power, and this power is what moves believers from talking the talk to walking the walk.

★ 5. Based on 4:20–21, what do you think Paul hoped to find when he visited Corinth? What would he find if he could visit you today?

DAY 3

1 Corinthians 5:1–13

READ 1 CORINTHIANS 5:1–13

Today's passage implies a mutual commitment among all members of a local church, suggesting this was standard in the early church. So although this passage is centered around an issue of sexual immorality, the *individual* who committed the act wasn't Paul's primary concern. Rather, the situation illustrated a bigger problem: moral compromise in the Corinthian church.

Review 5:1–2.

1. **Look up the phrase *sexual immorality* (5:1) in a Greek lexicon and write the definition below.**

When it came to sex, Greek culture was quite lenient; but in this case, a man was having relations with his stepmother, and even among Greeks this was viewed as wicked. Paul emphasized the issue by stating it occurred "among you," which highlighted his primary concern that such obscene behavior was being *accepted* within the Corinthian church.

2. Fill in the blanks in 5:2 below.

"And you are ________________! Ought you not rather to ____________? Let him who has done this be ________________ from among you."

Paul's phrase "not rather to mourn" revealed both the man's lack of repentance and the community's indifference. Their arrogance toward ongoing sin was an issue. (We know the sin was ongoing or habitual due to the verb tense Paul used in 5:1.)

3. Why might the church have allowed this practice? Why might the church have been arrogant instead of repentant and grieved by this behavior?

Review 5:3–5.

This was such a clear issue that Paul didn't need to be in person to respond; and he wanted them to know his message was in line with God's will. The goal of the discipline wasn't that the man would suffer for the rest of his life. Rather, the hope was that he'd experience conviction, repent, and return to the church. And as believers who are called to be ministers of reconciliation (2 Corinthians 2:5–7; 5:11), we can play a part in that trajectory.

4. To better understand Paul's recommendation for removing the unrepentant sinner, let's look at the words of Jesus. List the four steps Jesus provided in Matthew 18:15–20 for confronting a fellow believer who has sinned against you.

The church doesn't give or take away salvation. Only God can give salvation. However, this man's continued sin may have evidenced a lack of salvation to those observing his life—but no mere human could ever say for sure.

Review 5:6–8.

Paul clarified his teaching with two illustrations. First, he referenced the Passover feast. Typically, a pinch of old dough was used to leaven new batches of bread, but at Passover, the old dough was discarded to prevent harmful and poisonous fermentation that could build up over time (Exodus 12:15). Much like old leaven was removed, Paul wanted the church to remove the unrepentant sinner.

Then he shifted from the Passover feast's practice to its present-day significance: Christ fulfilled the law by dying for sin, defeating death, and offering salvation through faith, not works (Ephesians 2:8–9). Being a Christian doesn't make you sinless, but it should change your lifestyle over time.

★ 5. Read Romans 8:1 and James 5:16. Explain how Christians should respond when they sin. How do you typically respond when you sin?

Review 5:9–13.

Like you learned in the introduction, we don't know where 0 Corinthians is, but Paul aimed to clarify a part of it here. Some wrongly assumed he instructed Christians not to associate with nonbelievers, which was not the case. Christians shouldn't expect godly behavior from those who don't know God; instead, they should reach out with the gospel rather than judge.

Paul was urging the church to disconnect from immoral individuals who *identified* as Christians and had made *any* sin a pattern in their lives—with the hope they'd one day be reconciled and restored to fellowship. In 5:12, Paul made it clear that action was needed, and in 5:13 he told them what that action was.

6. There are various interpretations for what Paul may have intended in 5:13. Use a Bible study tool to find three of the possible views for how this purging of the "evil person" (unrepentant sinner) could've taken place and describe them below.

★ 7. Why is it a gift to gather with saints as the church? (See Hebrews 10:25 for help.)

DAY 4

1 Corinthians 6:1–11

READ 1 CORINTHIANS 6:1–11

Paul was astounded by the Corinthians' behavior. The issue he addressed in this passage is less about the legal system and more about (again) the failure of the local church to hold individual congregants accountable.

Review 6:1–3.

Much like with famous court cases today, Greek culture viewed anyone's legal battle as public entertainment; cases were even held at the Bema (judgment seat) in the town square. Paul was astonished Corinthian believers made themselves such a spectacle, unlike the Jews and other groups, who resolved their disputes privately.

1. What did Paul say in 6:2?

   A. Christians will judge the world with Christ.

   B. Christians aren't capable of settling disagreements.

   C. The cases being brought to the courts were too serious to address.

Paul wrote that Christians would one day judge angels, which is a rare mention of humanity's relation to angels in Scripture. Unlike people, who are created in God's image and will reign with Christ, angels weren't created in His image and won't reign with Him. (For greater clarity on this, look up Daniel 7:22 NLT and Jude 1:6 NKJV.)

Review 6:4–6.

Paul emphasized that any Christian in the church could help settle disputes, yet the Corinthians sought public courts. This was "to their shame" because, by going to court, they implied no one in the church—not even the Holy Spirit—could help. Their actions suggested they preferred justice from unbelievers over justice from their Spirit-filled brothers and sisters.

2. Read Acts 16:34–40. Do you think Paul was advocating for a complete prohibition of all legal action taken by Christians? Explain.

There was and still is a difference between civil cases (e.g., disagreements between parties like landlords and tenants) and criminal cases (e.g., governments prosecute crimes like murder or theft). Paul was addressing civil disputes that could've easily been settled in-house.

The Christians' casual acceptance of lawsuits damaged their witness. Remember Paul's main issue? He was more concerned by the behaviors the church tolerated (as they hurt their witness) than he was with the individuals who filed the lawsuits.

Review 6:7.

By suing each other, all the Corinthians involved had already lost. When Paul wrote, "Why not rather suffer wrong?" he meant it would've been better to settle disputes within the church, even if that meant an unfavorable outcome. Paul essentially said, *"Even if you've been wronged, you're doing more harm by going to court. You're damaging your witness."*

While we don't know the specifics of the conflicts Paul was addressing here, it's clear he was referring to multiple instances because "lawsuits" is plural. However, don't misunderstand the question "Why not rather suffer wrong?"—he wasn't suggesting staying in a physically unsafe situation (see Proverbs 27:12). These lawsuits seem to have more of a financial nature than a safety nature.

Review 6:8–11.

The Christians were cheating one another, which explains why they handled disputes poorly. Paul wasn't suggesting the ones who sued each other weren't true believers. He was making the point that faith should be followed by faithful actions. But because it wasn't, their actions naturally raised doubts about the genuineness of their faith.

Paul showed that cheating fellow believers was just as serious as any other sin. The inclusion of sexual immorality and homosexuality in his list was significant, because those behaviors were standard practice in the Roman Empire. The Corinthians were incredibly familiar with such issues, as their emperor, Nero, had castrated a boy and taken him as his "wife." Paul was essentially saying, "*Your deceitfulness in court is just as serious as Nero's sexual sin.*"

3. Look at the list of sins Paul provided in 6:9–10. Are there any sins you tend to believe are worse than others? Is your thinking correct? Explain.

What's the answer or solution to all these sins and their consequences? Jesus! Paul reminded the Corinthians who they were before Christ (notice he used past tense words even though they were presently misbehaving); but he also put the power of the gospel on display.

4. Based on 6:11, the Corinthians were washed, sanctified, and justified. Using a Bible dictionary or study Bible, define the terms in the table below.

Washing (Regeneration)	Sanctification	Justification

DAY 5

1 Corinthians 6:12–20

READ 1 CORINTHIANS 6:12–20

Review 6:12.

Paul responded to the Corinthians' questions about sex, challenging the idea that "all things are lawful" (possibly a cultural saying or a quote from a previous letter). He emphasized that what was allowed wasn't always fruitful.

Review 6:13–14.

The Corinthians probably used logic suggesting that just like they had physical appetites, they had sexual ones. They probably said, *"It's natural. What's the issue?"* But Paul argued that God didn't create us to desire distorted sexual relations. Hunger—both physical and spiritual—points to our need for and dependence on God. We have a longing for Him that was distorted when sin separated us from Him.

★ 1. What worldly things have you attempted to use to satisfy a longing (or hunger) only God can fill? Explain.

People have inherent value because they're made in God's image (Genesis 1:27). God's image can be represented through our actions, thoughts, and intellect, but it can also be represented physically. For example, God raised Jesus up in a physical body.

Review 6:15–17.

Some Corinthians likely thought their sexual activity was separate from their spiritual lives. But when one person sinned, especially through sexual immorality, it dishonored the whole body of Christ.

Because married couples become "one flesh" through sex and because the Corinthians belonged to Christ, they had no right to give themselves to anyone outside their marriage.

2. Fill in the blanks in 6:16 below.

"Or do you not know that he who is ____________ to a ______________ becomes ______ body with her? For, as it is written, 'The ______ will become ______ flesh.'"

Knowing the Corinthians' questions from their letter to him, Paul defined God's original design for sex (before sin entered the picture) by quoting Genesis 2:24. Prostitution was a common and casual practice in Greek culture, but Paul made this clear: Casual sex is never casual.

Paul emphasized the deep oneness believers share with Christ, which is even stronger than the oneness married couples experience through intercourse. But think about the implications of this truth. If a believer is first one with Christ and then has sex with a prostitute, what kind of dishonorable messages are their actions sending Him?

Review 6:18–20.

3. Look back at our study of 5:1. The same Greek word Paul used for "sexual immorality" is used here. What was the word and what does it mean?

Paul issued a clear command that likely called to mind Joseph fleeing from Potiphar's wife (Genesis 39:7–20); he encouraged the Corinthians to make a habit of actively fleeing sexual immorality. But make no mistake, Paul encouraged them to flee sexual *immorality*, not sex in general. Sex within the boundaries of marriage is a good gift from God.

4. In 6:18, what did Paul say the sexually immoral person sins against?

This phrase teaches that sexual immorality has unique effects and consequences. Back in 1 Corinthians 3, Paul stated that the broader church is a temple. In 6:19, he explained that this sin impacts not only the collective body, but also the individual.

When believers place their faith in Christ, God's Spirit dwells in them. This gift of the Spirit to new covenant believers can't be taken away, but the Spirit who dwells in us *can* be grieved (Ephesians 4:30). We grieve the Spirit when we respond to His direction with disobedience or delay. Paul taught the Corinthians to glorify God with their bodies because He lives in them and they belong to Him.

★ 5. How do these verses intersect with your life? What might God be saying to you?

You might read 6:20 and think, *I failed*. But please remember those failures were paid for by Christ on the cross. God's forgiveness isn't a license to sin, but it certainly offers freedom from guilt and shame. Praise God that His mercies are new every morning! He's where the joy is!

6. What stood out to you most in this week's study? Why?

7. What did you learn or relearn about God and His character this week?

DAY 6

Corresponding Psalm & Prayer

READ PSALM 7

1. What correlation do you see between Psalm 7 and this week's study?

2. What portions of this psalm stand out to you most?

3. Close by praying this prayer aloud:

Father,

Your mercies are new every morning. You wash us, You sanctify us, and You justify us. You are righteous and I praise Your name!

I haven't met Your standards for righteousness when it comes to sexuality or any element of your moral law. I've tried to satisfy my hunger for You with selfish actions. I've dismissed my own sin as minor. And I've been overly harsh—or passively indifferent—toward the sin of those around me. Like the Corinthians, I've promoted myself to be judge and even king. But like David wrote, I know that You are the judge.

Test my heart, God, and reveal any hidden sin so that I can repent of it. Make me both a servant of Christ and a steward of the mysteries of God. Grant me a kingdom mindset. Help me not just talk the talk, but walk the walk. Help me look like Jesus.

I surrender my life to You, Lord—every moment of my day, each decision I make, I yield my will and way to Your perfect will and way.

I love You too. Amen.

DAY 7

Rest, Catch Up, or Dig Deeper

WEEKLY CHALLENGE

In 1 Corinthians 5, Paul addressed a matter of church discipline. Many believe this chapter makes a case for formal church membership. Spend some time researching your home church's or a local church's approach to these topics.

- How is your church's leadership system structured?
- How do they view or practice church discipline?
- Is there anything else you're curious about?

You may need to consult their website to find answers to these questions. (If you're unable to find the answers you're seeking, feel free to request a meeting with a church staff member.) Take notes on what you learn.

WEEK 3

1 Corinthians 7–9

Scripture to Memorize

If I give away all I have,
and if I deliver up my body
to be burned, but have
not love, I gain nothing.
1 Corinthians 13:3

DAILY BIBLE READING

Day 1: 1 Corinthians 7:1–16

Day 2: 1 Corinthians 7:17–24

Day 3: 1 Corinthians 7:25–40

Day 4: 1 Corinthians 8:1–13

Day 5: 1 Corinthians 9:1–27

Day 6: Psalm 39

Day 7: Catch-Up Day

Corresponds to Days 334 and 335 of *The Bible Recap*.

WEEKLY CHALLENGE

See page 80 for more information.

DAY 1

1 Corinthians 7:1–16

READ 1 CORINTHIANS 7:1–16

Throughout his letters, Paul taught early churches how to uphold the Christian sexual ethic and how to have God-honoring marriages. Here, in response to a question raised by the Corinthian church, he addressed both topics, contending that a husband and wife should honor each other with sex.

Review 7:1–2.

1. What phrase in 7:1 lets us know Paul was referring to the Corinthians' letter to him? What issue here had they written to him about?

Because God's good gift of sex had been so twisted in first-century Corinth, some Christians there seem to have decided to avoid sex altogether, even if they were married. This could've been a noble—but misguided—attempt to be holy, setting themselves apart from the depraved culture around them. Or this could've been an arrogant way to appear *holier than thou*, showing off as people who were so spiritual that they had transcended their sexual desires. Either way, it wasn't God's plan for marriage and sex. Enduring Word's commentary explains that as much as Satan wants sex outside of marriage to be rampant, he wants sex inside of marriage to be nonexistent.[1] God's plan puts sex where it belongs and where it should thrive: in marriage.

Review 7:3–5.

2. Who did Paul address first in this section? Summarize three of his teachings about marriage and sex from 7:3–5.

It's nothing new that the world tries to portray the Christian sexual ethic as antiquated and oppressive. Similar accusations have been made since the beginning of Christianity. But Paul was actually doing something radical here. In a culture where women had very little legal or societal authority, he presented the husband and the wife as equals, with equal marital and physical rights. What Paul said about one spouse here, he said about the other.

Of course, sometimes circumstances, such as health issues, can make sex difficult or even impossible. Paul's teachings on marriage and sex must never be used as a justification for sexual coercion, but rather an encouragement for shared affection and intimacy. Both husbands and wives have God-given sexual desires, and whenever possible, both spouses can (and should!) fulfill each other's needs with mutual respect and love.

Review 7:6–9.

In this section, Paul begins to use a literary tool he rarely employs elsewhere: distinguishing his own teachings from God's commands. (Note: It might be helpful to circle the clarifying statements in your Bible to see this more clearly.) He continued this process throughout the rest of this chapter. He willingly shared the wisdom he'd gained from his own experiences—which is valuable in its own right—but he made sure to separate it from Old Testament laws and the teachings of Jesus.

Paul noted that both singleness and marriage are gifts from God, and the Giver is the one who chooses what gift to give.

★ 3. Ask God to help you view your marital status as truly a gift from Him, then list some of the benefits of singleness and marriage in the chart below.

Singleness	Marriage

4. Review 7:8–9. What did Paul say to the unmarried and widowed Corinthian Christians in these verses?

Be careful not to build a theology around this statement alone. Paul didn't fully unpack here why he instructed the single believers in Corinth this way, but he'll circle back to this by the end of this chapter. Stay tuned.

Review 7:10–11.

5. Complete the table below.

Passage	Teacher	Instructions to Husbands	Instructions to Wives	Any Concessions?
Matthew 5:32				
Mark 10:11–12				
1 Corinthians 7:10–11				

Review 7:12–13.

Don't mistake Paul's guidance here as justification for a believer to marry an unbeliever. The first-century Christian church had many believers whose spouses had not converted. Arranged marriages were also common. Paul's gentle encouragement to Christian spouses who were already married to non-Christians was this: Endure.

Review 7:14–16.

★ 6. Why did Paul encourage the believing spouse to endure in their marriage?

Unbelievers aren't saved by proximity to believers, but throughout the history of the church, many have been drawn to Him through the faithful day-to-day witness of believing parents, grandparents, friends, and spouses.

However, Paul did note that if an unbelieving spouse left their marriage, then the believing spouse was "free." Some theologians believe this means they are free to remarry, while other theologians believe this means they are simply free from that marriage but must remain single.[2] Regardless of your convictions about what divorced Christians are free *to* or *from*, we can say with certainty what God has called all Christians to: peace (7:15). That peace isn't trite or hollow. It's the peace that comes from a right relationship with God and a pursuit of holiness.

So Paul, with the care of a pastor, encouraged believers to endure in their marriages, and even to have hope. After all, as Paul reminded us all in 7:16, who knows what God will do or how He'll use you to be a part of it?

DAY 2

1 Corinthians 7:17–24

READ 1 CORINTHIANS 7:17–24

Paul specified that his teaching in this section of his letter wasn't Corinth-specific, but rather applicable to all the churches he ministered to. What he wrote here falls under the banner of "his teachings" (beginning in 7:6 from yesterday's study) but remains helpful and encouraging for us today.

Review 7:17.

★ 1. According to 7:17, what was the main theme of Paul's teaching in this section?

In the middle of teaching about singleness, sex, and marriage, Paul seemed to veer off course. But he wasn't just sidetracked by a couple of tangents; rather, he used two examples to teach the Corinthians that they already understood his central point.

Review 7:18–20.

2. In Paul's first example, what doesn't count? What does count?

Circumcision was a part of the covenant God made with Abraham (Genesis 17:1–14). For generations, it set God's family (Jews) apart from those around them. Once Christ fulfilled the Old Testament law, circumcision was no longer required (Acts 15:1–11; Romans 4:9–11).

However, in the early days of the church, when many men in first-century Corinth would have gone to public baths and participated in sports in the nude, circumcision was a heavily debated issue. So some new Gentile (non-Jew) Christians decided they needed to be circumcised. And some Jewish Christians decided they needed to be "uncircumcised." (And if you're thinking that's impossible, let's just say a medical procedure was available, even back then.)[1]

Under the old covenant, circumcision was outward and physical. Under the new covenant, circumcision was inward and metaphorical (Romans 2:28–29). Here, Paul reminded believers what mattered was having genuine beliefs and living them out. And that can be accomplished without ever changing your body.

In 1:26, Paul taught about Christians' *calling* as an overarching principle that applies to all Christians, in every place, in every time. The same is true here: Whether Jew or Gentile, rich or poor, man or woman, single or married, a Christian's calling is to love the Lord our God with all our hearts, souls, and minds and to love our neighbors as ourselves (Matthew 22:37–39).

Review 7:21–23.

3. In Paul's second example, what did he say to Christian bondservants? What did he say to freedmen?

In the first century, being a bondservant—sometimes translated as "slave"—was typically a temporary situation in which someone would submit themselves to work to repay a debt. Being a bondservant likely wasn't anyone's dream job, but it wasn't at all similar to the systems of enslavement that we're familiar with today. Some bondservants in the first century even continued working for their former masters after they'd bought their freedom.

Review 7:24.

4. Fill in the blanks in 7:24 below.

"So, brothers, in ______________ ________________ each was

___________, there let him ___________ ________ ______."

As Paul wrapped up these two examples, he reiterated the point he was illustrating: Wherever you were when God called you to Himself, and wherever He has placed you now, He is with you. Salvation is life-changing because it is heart-changing. But—sometimes to our disappointment or frustration—it may not necessarily be circumstance-changing. Salvation changes our position before God, but not necessarily our condition on earth.

Because today's two examples applied to a specific audience, and because the principle applies to us all, it's important to be clear about what Paul was *not* saying here. This passage isn't an excuse for a single Christian to keep living with their girlfriend or boyfriend. And this passage isn't telling a Christian in an abusive relationship to stay in it.

But to those who long for a higher income or a more fulfilling job or a bigger home or different physical circumstances or a spouse, know this: You're not in the wrong place. You don't have to wait until your condition in life changes to serve Him better or more fully. Wherever you are, He has called you. Wherever you are, thanks be to God, *He is with you.*

★ 5. What conditions have you been hoping would change? How does it bring you comfort that God remains with you?

DAY 3

1 Corinthians 7:25–40

 READ 1 CORINTHIANS 7:25–40

Here again, Paul differentiates his teachings—even though they are filled with wisdom and encouragement—from God's commands and the teachings of Christ. When he began this section with "now concerning the betrothed" (7:25), he referred to another part of the letter they'd written to him. There's not an absolute agreement among theologians as to what Paul addressed here, but it's likely that he was referring to the practice of arranged marriage, instructing engaged couples who were wondering if they should get married after all.[1]

Regardless of the exact question Paul answered here, we can be sure that—as with any biblical passage—ignoring the original context and audience is dangerous. And we can be sure that—as with any biblical passage—throwing the passage out the window, insisting it doesn't apply to us, is also dangerous. Let's strive to be faithful readers of God's Word and avoid both.

Review 7:25.

As he's done several times in this chapter, he made a point to tell the Corinthian Christians that what he wrote next was his own judgment but that it was trustworthy.

★ 1. Why was Paul's judgment "trustworthy" (7:25)? Use what you've learned so far in this study to make your case.

Review 7:26–28.

Paul wrote a new verse of the same song: "There let him remain with God" (7:24) became "it is good for a person to remain as he is" (7:26). And he said that this was specifically due to "the present distress" (7:26).

There was *plenty* of distress to choose from when Paul wrote. The newly formed Christian church, walking on wobbly toddler legs, was finding its way while surviving a famine and hearing disturbing reports of persecution.[2] In the first-century Roman Empire, Christians were captured, tortured, and murdered. Some were fed to wild animals, while others were burned alive as human torches. And sometimes, family members—husbands, wives, and children—were forced to watch all of this happen to their loved ones. When a first-century Christian was single, persecution was no less real or horrific. But it seems Paul wished to spare as many as possible from the unique torture of witnessing the persecution of their spouse and children.[3]

Review 7:29–31.

2. What did Paul address in this section? (Refer to 7:29 and 7:31 for help finding the main idea.)

Paul didn't promise his readers that Jesus would be back in their lifetime. But he encouraged them to live as if He would be. Throughout his letters, Paul urged the church to be faithful in both their daily decisions—like what they ate—and in their big decisions—like whether to marry. They were to live up to their calling above all else, because "the present form of this world is passing away" (7:31). To the first-century Christian facing famine and possible persecution, these were words of comfort, peace, and hope.

★ 3. What does it mean to you as a Christian that the present form of this world is passing away?

Review 7:32–35.

4. Keeping in mind the context and original audience of 1 Corinthians, check all of the following statements that are true based on 7:32–35.

- ☐ Paul wanted to spare the Corinthian Christians from as much anxiety as possible.
- ☐ Married people are concerned about their spouses.
- ☐ Single people don't have anything to worry about.
- ☐ Married people have fewer opportunities to serve God.
- ☐ Single people have more time to serve God.
- ☐ Paul wanted to restrict the Corinthian Christians from having a good time.

Review 7:36–40.

Paul reiterated that getting married wasn't sinful. In fact, he said that those who marry "do well" (7:37). Married Christians weren't wrong in being concerned about their spouses. Remember, Paul spent the better part of eleven verses at the beginning of this chapter instructing people to honor their spouses with attention and affection. But here, he said that those who remain single "do even better" (7:38). Paul's teaching here to the first-century Corinthian Christians doesn't seem to be about right and wrong, but about good and better. His words likely served as a great encouragement to the single Christians in Corinth, who lived in a culture where marriage signaled a higher status.

As we wrap up this chapter, let's review some of what we studied.

5. Complete the table below.

Paul's Teachings to First-Century Corinthian Christians on Singleness, Marriage, and Divorce

	If . . .	Then . . .
7:9	a single or widowed person can't exercise self-control	
7:10–11	you separate	
7:12–13	you have an unbelieving spouse, and they stay	
7:15	the unbelieving spouse leaves the marriage	
7:27	you are married	
7:27	you are single	
7:39	a wife's husband dies	

6. Which of these teachings do you think apply to believers today? Why?

DAY 4

1 Corinthians 8:1–13

READ 1 CORINTHIANS 8:1–13

Eating food that had been offered to idols was such a big issue in first-century churches that they invented a word for it: *eidōlothytos*.[1]

In pagan temples, after animals were offered as sacrifices to various idols, the meat was sometimes eaten in ceremonies in the temples as a continuation of the idol worship. So it seems that the easy solution would've been to avoid the pagan temple altogether, and Paul addressed that in 8:10. But the line got blurry, because some of the meat that had been offered as an idol sacrifice was then sold in markets. Market vendors often sold this meat cheaply,[2] and because there was a famine, it might've been the only affordable meat available.

Review 8:1–3.

When Paul wrote "all of us possess knowledge," he was likely quoting their letter back to them again—but it wasn't a compliment. He basically said, "*Yeah, we all know about what's happening with the market meat. But you're using your knowledge and missing the entire point. You're letting it inflate your ego.*"

★ 1. What's the difference between puffing up and building up? How did it apply to *eidōlothytos*? How does it apply today?

Knowledge is good, and seeking knowledge of God is a worthy—and lifelong—pursuit (Psalm 19:2; Proverbs 1:7; Romans 11:33). But seeking knowledge for the sake of knowledge is hollow. And insisting that you have all the knowledge you need is foolish. Puffed-up knowledge without built-up love is dangerous. It can lead to dogmatism and legalism, or it can lead to flippancy and licentiousness.

2. To which extreme did the Corinthian Christians' puffed-up knowledge seem to lead them?

A. Legalism

B. Licentiousness

Review 8:4–6.

Again, Paul quoted their letter back to them: Their "knowledge" was that "an idol has no real existence." Paul didn't disagree that the pagan idols were made by human hands, and he didn't disagree with their understanding that there is one true God. But it's noteworthy that in 8:5, Paul wrote, "For although there may be so-called gods in heaven or on earth—as indeed there are many 'gods' and many 'lords' . . ." These other gods and lords exist. In fact, other passages in Scripture indicate they might be demonic forces (Deuteronomy 32:16–17; Leviticus 17:7; 1 Corinthians 10:20). But they are absolutely nothing in comparison to the Lord of Lords.

3. Fill in the blanks in 8:6 to remind you who the one true God is.

". . . yet for us there is ______ ______, ______ ____________, from whom are ______ ____________ and for whom ______ ____________, and ______ ________, __________ ____________, through whom are ______ ____________ and through whom ______ __________."

Review 8:7–8.

Yes, God made everything, *including* the animal that was sacrificed to an idol. And to that, Paul essentially said, "*But here's the thing: Not all of you know this.*" In their church, many believers came from a pagan background, and they had only just left it. Probably many of their family members and friends were still pagan. Paul said their consciences were weak. And what's key in understanding this passage (and much of this letter) is that he didn't admonish the weak—he admonished the ones who were puffed up in their knowledge.

Paul agreed that the *eidōlothytos* itself wasn't the problem. The problem was that it was causing their brothers and sisters to stumble.

Review 8:9–13.

4. What did Paul call their freedom to eat *eidōlothytos* in 8:9?

Rights come with responsibilities, and this is especially true in the Christian life. Unknowingly causing a brother or sister to stumble in their faith is thoughtless and immature. *Knowingly* causing a brother or sister to stumble in their faith is sin. We would never leave a physical obstacle in the direct path of someone with a disability; we would remove it from their path. And we certainly would never *place* an obstacle there. Why would we do so with spiritual matters?

★ 5. What are some examples of spiritual obstacles Christians place in the path of their weaker siblings?

★ 6. How should we balance our rights and freedoms in Christ with our responsibilities to His church?

DAY 5

1 Corinthians 9:1–27

READ 1 CORINTHIANS 9:1–27

Paul's writing style can be difficult for modern, Western readers to follow. He included lots of *digressions*, which were a common tool in Greek rhetoric. For many of us today, these short topic shifts can be confusing. But for his original audience, digressions strengthened his argument.[1] So as you read Paul's letters, a helpful practice is to keep zooming out and reminding yourself of the main topic.

1. What was the main topic that Paul had just written about in 1 Corinthians 8? What was its broader implication? (Refer to 8:1 and 8:13 if needed.)

Review 9:1–3.

Here, Paul reminded the Corinthians of his own calling and freedoms. The Corinthian church itself verified Paul's authenticity as an apostle. And as an apostle, Paul had certain rights.

Review 9:4–14.

2. What were Paul's rights that he listed here?

Using common occupations as examples, Paul set up his argument that apostles had the right to be supported by the church for the work they were doing for the gospel: Soldiers were paid for their service, vineyard workers ate the fruit of their labor, shepherds drank milk from the flock.

So if all of that was agreed upon as right, then Paul argued that this should also be true: Apostles should be supported in their labor for the kingdom. What's more, Paul pointed out, is that the Old Testament law said the same thing (Leviticus 6:16, 26; Numbers 5:9–10; Deuteronomy 18:1). *"And even more than that,"* Paul continued, *"Jesus Himself said that those who preach the gospel should be supported by those who receive it"* (Matthew 10:10; Luke 10:7).

Review 9:15–18.

3. What's the connection between Paul's main topic now and *eidōlothytos* in 1 Corinthians 8?

Paul said the reason that he gave up his right to a wage was so he wouldn't be deprived of his "ground for boasting" (9:15). You may be thinking, *Wait a minute, Paul—why are you boasting at all?*

4. Read Romans 15:17–19. Why was Paul boasting?

Review 9:19–23.

If you've heard a brother or sister use 9:22, you've likely heard them use it out of context as a justification to be in a place they probably shouldn't be or as an excuse for acting in a way they probably shouldn't act. But Paul's point here was the exact opposite: His freedoms in Christ were great, but he willingly laid them down to become a servant.

Becoming "all things to all people" (9:22) doesn't mean that we are chameleons who can blend in with the world as easily as we can blend in with our church pew. Becoming all things to all people means that—like Paul—we look at our own rights and freedoms and say, "Even though I can, that doesn't mean I should."

5. Complete the table below with some of the rights or freedoms that Paul gave up for the sake of the gospel.

1 Corinthians 8:12–13	
1 Corinthians 9:4–15	
Galatians 5:13	
Acts 18:18	

The Corinthians were so busy insisting on the rights they had in Christ that they lost sight of Christ Himself—the one who gave up His rights for them.

★ 6. Read Philippians 2:3–8. What rights did Christ give up? For whom?

★ 7. How does this shape your understanding of your rights?

Review 9:24–27.

As Paul wrapped up this section, he digressed once more. Corinth was home to the Isthmian Games, second only in popularity to the Olympics.[2] Athletes, he reminded them, needed extreme discipline. They didn't just train in their specific sport. Their training impacted every area of their lives—what they ate, what they drank, when they slept, and more. And all of that was for a fleeting moment of glory—a wreath that would dry up and crumble.

Paul wasn't advocating for a works-based salvation. But a changed heart is shown by a changed life, and true understanding of salvation is marked by genuine acts of service and love. The prize we've been given—which will be made complete when Christ returns—is eternal.

He is our prize, and He's where the joy is!

8. What stood out to you most in this week's study? Why?

9. What did you learn or relearn about God and His character this week?

DAY 6

Corresponding Psalm & Prayer

READ PSALM 39

1. What correlation do you see between Psalm 39 and this week's study?

2. What portions of this psalm stand out to you most?

3. Close by praying this prayer aloud:

Father,

You are greater than I can fully understand. From everlasting to everlasting, You were and are and always will be. I am fleeting, but You are forever.

You've placed me where I am as a gift, but I have seen it as a punishment. And so I've tried desperately to trade my gift and change my position. Forgive me. You've called me to peace and love, but I've been too busy insisting that I have rights and freedoms. And so I have caused my weaker siblings to stumble. Forgive me.

Like David, teach me to measure my days. Let me remain where I am, secure with You. Like Paul, teach me to be all things to all people. Help me give up my freedoms in order to reach others for You.

This world is passing away, and I am a sojourner here, just like all who have gone before me. Knowing that, I surrender my life to You, Lord—every moment of my day, each decision I make, I yield my will and way to Your perfect will and way.

I love You too. Amen.

DAY 7

Rest, Catch Up, or Dig Deeper

In 1 Corinthians 8–9, Paul urged the church to give up some of their freedoms for the sake of the gospel. Is there a freedom (or freedoms) God is leading you to give up? It could be a freedom that is hindering your witness for Christ, or it could be a freedom that is hindering your growth in Christ. Write out a prayer of surrender and ask God for help in this area.

WEEK 4

1 Corinthians 10–11

Scripture to Memorize

Love is patient and kind; love does not envy or boast; it is not arrogant or rude. It does not insist on its own way; it is not irritable or resentful; it does not rejoice at wrongdoing, but rejoices with the truth.

1 Corinthians 13:4–6

DAILY BIBLE READING

Day 1: 1 Corinthians 10:1–13
Day 2: 1 Corinthians 10:14–22
Day 3: 1 Corinthians 10:23–33
Day 4: 1 Corinthians 11:1–16
Day 5: 1 Corinthians 11:17–34
Day 6: Psalm 16
Day 7: Catch-Up Day

Corresponds to Day 335 of *The Bible Recap*.

WEEKLY CHALLENGE

See page 101 for more information.

DAY 1

1 Corinthians 10:1–13

1 CORINTHIANS 10:1–13

Review 10:1–6.

As Paul sets out here to warn the Corinthians against idolatry, he reminds them of a story many (specifically the Jewish converts to Christianity) would have been familiar with. The Israelites had a spiritual experience and direct encounters with God, yet they still failed to enter the promised land. Paul wasn't talking about salvation in this section of the letter. He was, in response to current events, warning the Corinthian church not to miss out on the fullness of what God had for them.

Paul pointed out that the fact that the Corinthian Christians had been baptized and had taken Communion didn't guarantee they were living in ways that pleased God. In the same way, passing through the Red Sea (Exodus 14) and eating God's miraculous provision of manna in the wilderness (Exodus 16) didn't mean that the Israelites—who had indeed been delivered from Egypt—would make it to the promised land God had awaiting them.

1. True or false: In this passage, Paul was saying that the presence of miracles is enough to let us know we're pleasing God.

Bible scholars debate as to whether 10:4 implies a literal rock or a stream followed the Israelites. But the point is the same in either case: Jesus was with Israel in the wilderness. Paul made sure to note that fact to the Corinthian Christians, lest they think that because they had Jesus, this metaphor didn't apply to them.

Despite all this blessing and supernatural provision, "most of" the Israelites did not please God.

2. According to Numbers 14:38, how many men from the adult generation that left Egypt came into the promised land?

That's out of 603,550 who originally left Egypt (Numbers 1:46). And that's only counting the men, as was common in census-taking measures of the time. Almost *all* of them never entered into what God had available for them—something far better than the temporary satiations of the desires they'd chased in the wilderness. God's ways are not about self-denial unto its own end. Jesus came that we might have life, and have it more abundantly (see John 10:10).

3. Write a prayer asking God to help you "not desire evil as they did" (10:6) but to increasingly walk in fullness with God.

Review 10:7–13.

"Rose up to play" refers to the sexual activity and orgy-like behavior that took place in pagan idol worship—both in Exodus 32:6 and in Corinthian times. Paul was defining idolatry by the sexual immorality that popped up in various forms throughout history.

★ 4. You may have never attended a party for Poseidon or bowed down to a statue, but there are things we give allegiance to that serve as modern-day versions of these idols. What do you think those might be in your own life?

The Corinthian Christians may have thought they were safe from the danger of being destroyed because of the spiritual experiences they'd had. But Paul warned that if the Israelites were punished in this way, the Corinthians could be too.

Along that same line, when Paul mentioned not putting Christ to the test, he wasn't referring to asking legitimate questions with an earnest heart. He was talking about seeing how much we can get away with when it comes to sin. This kind of thinking is missing the promised land way of life.

The irony here is that the prideful are most prone to missing the warning, and thus, the most in danger of repeating the Israelites' mistakes. The enemy loves to make us think we're the only one who has encountered *this specific temptation* under *these specific circumstances*. But Paul said all temptation is common. God always provides a way of escape, and we'll never be given temptation beyond what we can handle. (Note: 10:13 does *not* say we'll never be given *circumstances* beyond what we can handle. We often will, but He promises help there too.)

★ 5. Briefly describe a time when God helped you resist temptation.

DAY 2

1 Corinthians 10:14–22

 READ 1 CORINTHIANS 10:14–22

Review 10:14–15.

Paul began this section both lovingly and firmly. He called the Corinthian Christians "beloved"—but he also said to *flee*.

1. Which of the following do you think Paul meant by "flee"?

   A. Eventually see if you can slowly extricate yourself when it's convenient.

   B. Go, but slowly, so it's not awkward.

   C. Run away from a place or situation God said to avoid.

Up to this point in his letter, Paul has discussed guidelines about eating meat sacrificed to idols. He's also discussed places where more of a principled, heart-focused approach was appropriate in guiding Christian decisions in this idol-drenched culture.

But in today's passage, Paul discussed a very specific event-based element of this idolatry question: Was it okay for Christians to attend banquets that were being put on in honor of idols? These may have been events the Corinthians wrote to Paul to ask about, or he may have just known that some in the church were attending them.

Their culture considered itself enlightened. And Paul doubly appealed to their cultural sensibilities—speaking sarcastically and appealing to their hubris as Greeks, who liked to believe they were logically and intellectually superior to others. He basically said, "*You consider yourself rational. Then you should be able to recognize this as a rational argument, right?*"

Paul said they, as sensible people, had the responsibility and ability to receive the sensible thing he was about to say. Perhaps he anticipated some pushback. Perhaps these events were quite popular and he knew some Christians might not be ready to give them up.

Review 10:16–22.

With his rhetoric established, Paul explained why these banquet events were prohibited. He also clarified why this mandate was distinct from what he had previously said about eating food sacrificed to idols. In this passage, he wasn't discussing food—he was discussing an event.

2. What is the cup of blessing, also known as the cup of praise? **Use a Bible study tool for your research and write what you find.**

This was the cup Jesus blessed at the Last Supper with His disciples, indicating that it was the "new covenant in my blood" (Luke 22:20). Paul was making the point that the Corinthian Christians were covenanting with Christ when they participated in Communion.

Likewise, in the ancient world, eating at the same table with someone was significant. To eat of one loaf of bread was to be of one body. Paul asked this rhetorical question: When the priests in Israel ate the holy sacrifices as God directed, was that not an act of fellowship with God?

3. True or false: According to 10:19–20, Paul was implying that idols or food offered to idols were significant in and of themselves.

Paul said demonic spirits enslaved people through idol worship. Though the idols themselves were nothing more than wood or stone, the demonic spirits behind those idols were to whom those sacrifices were being offered. And they should flee from any alliance with demons.

If there was meaning behind eating at the Lord's Table in Communion—which the Corinthian Christians knew there to be—then there was also spiritual significance in eating at the table of demons.

Based on 10:22, it seems perhaps some of these Corinthian Christians were eating at pagan tables under the justification of being "such strong Christians that they could handle it."

★ 4. Is there an area of your life where you've rationalized feeling "strong enough" to participate, but perhaps, in truth, participation in this area leads to disunity and broken fellowship with God?

★ 5. What would it look like to change that area of your life?

The question behind our decision-making as Christians is not just "Is this harmful for *me*?" God is a relational God. Eating at those tables was an act of fellowship with the enemies of God—and the enemies of our soul. That's an RSVP *no*.

DAY 3

1 Corinthians 10:23–33

 READ 1 CORINTHIANS 10:23–33

Review 10:23–24.

As you learned in your study of 1 Corinthians 6:12, "all things are lawful" may have been a common saying at the time, or it may have been a specific quote Paul was responding to from their previous letter. He wasn't really saying all things are pleasing to God or all things are permissible. He was challenging their thinking and pointing out that what was *allowed* was not the same thing as what was *fruitful*.

Review 10:25–33.

The fact that there may have been a famine at the time could be why Paul got so specific here. When he quoted Psalm 24, he was telling them not to worry at the market: The food itself is not the issue—for it belongs to God, the Creator.

You learned in 1 Corinthians 8 that a lot of people in this church came out of a pagan culture, and eating meat sacrificed to idols was part of their old way of life. So Paul's teaching in this section explained that, while the meat itself was not the issue, the relational elements of eating the meat did matter.

If an unbeliever invited them to dinner, they could eat what was provided. The guiding principle was this: *Don't waste the dinner debating* eidōlothytos *with them. It's about the time together in community.*

But if the believer knew the meat was sacrificed to idols and they ate it anyway, that might be confusing to a new believer trying to understand how to navigate *eidōlothytos*. Or it might be a stumbling block to another Christian who thought that action was wrong.

Paul wasn't being inconsistent here. His guiding principle was the same throughout: freedom with the limitations of love.

1. Which of the following was Paul saying in 10:29–30?

A. Become a slave to other people's opinions.

B. Food, in and of itself, is the issue.

C. We are free in Jesus, so maximizing our personal freedoms is the ultimate goal.

D. None of the above.

It's not uncommon to prefer a clear set of rules, listed out detail by detail. It seems that may have been what the Corinthian Christians were asking for. But what God reveals to us about His heart in Scripture—and what Paul pointed to in this passage—is that "the kingdom of God is not a matter of eating and drinking, but of righteousness and peace and joy in the Holy Spirit" (Romans 14:17). The Holy Spirit gives us invaluable discernment in situations when the appropriate response isn't obvious.

Paul's famous statement in verse 31 provides a partial summary for chapter 10 and is a great guiding principle for all the questions he was answering for the Corinthians. He essentially said, "*In every area you asked about, act for the glory of God.*" If that's our aim, a lot of other questions fall away.

★ **2. Write down some areas of your life you'd like to commit to the glory of God.**

So whether I __________ or __________ or __________, or whatever I do, do all to the glory of God.

★ **3. What would it look like to make adjustments in your thinking or liberties to apply the above to your life?**

4. Circle all the parties Paul told the Corinthian Christians to "give no offense" to (10:32).

Only other Christians | Only nonbelievers | Only those in leadership

Jews and Greeks and the church of God | Only official church members

Paul was clear that the Corinthian Christians were to consider both those *in* the church and those outside of it. It's worth noting, however, that he wasn't talking about not offending the *legalism* of other believers. Throughout his letters, he was often bold about correcting legalism (Galatians 5:11–12 offers a particularly potent example).

And in that same vein, Paul wasn't talking about becoming a people pleaser—though it's hard to imagine him being accused of such. The desire he expressed in this passage was that these Corinthians would put aside their own desires to serve the good of the whole.

5. Why did he follow that advice himself, according to 10:33?

DAY 4

1 Corinthians 11:1–16

READ 1 CORINTHIANS 11:1–16

Review 11:1–2.

In Corinthian culture, students learned from their teachers by imitating them, and Paul didn't shy away from that responsibility. He wasn't saying, *"Look how amazing I am."* He was embracing the responsibility he had as a leader and teacher, trying to walk in a way that imitated Christ, and telling the Corinthian Christians to do the same.

In 11:2, he was likely being sarcastic—because they did *not* remember him in everything and were selective in the teachings they chose to uphold. And he was going to correct them. Throughout this letter he's been correcting things going on in their church and responding to things they asked about in their letter to him. It's important to remember that as we read this next section, which may challenge our modern sensibilities.

Paul wasn't laying out dogma in this passage. He was correcting chaos—chaos that had been happening in this specific church as Corinthians continued to make choices that compromised the spread of the gospel.

This passage is not a comprehensive summary of God's viewpoint on men and women. For that, we would need to look at the entirety of Scripture.

As we saw in our study of 1 Corinthians 7, there's danger in not incorporating context into our reading of certain passages, and there's danger in throwing out the passage *because* of the context. Jesus Christ is the same yesterday, today, and forever (Hebrews 13:8). But culture changes all the time, and cultural differences can certainly be a challenge in the Christian walk.

1. Write down any fears or concerns you have about today's passage. Knowing God cares about all these details, ask Him to lead you to any healing or helpful truth He may have for you in His Word today.

Review 11:3–16.

There are a few different views about what this passage might mean (and whether certain aspects still apply). As a reminder, this passage isn't a full teaching on men and women, or husbands and wives. With the information we have about the particular scenario Paul was addressing, it seems some wives were publicly behaving in ways that were dishonoring to their husbands—perhaps a modern comparison would be not wearing a wedding ring. Paul aimed to correct this behavior to bring unity and clarity.

Note Paul's mention of women praying and prophesying. This was a big deal. Head coverings were *common* in this culture; but women praying and prophesying was countercultural. And this was true for so many areas of the early church, where Jesus had elevated women in a culture that often viewed them as little more than property. A woman's word didn't even count as legitimate testimony in court at that time.

But it was a woman whom Jesus first chose to reveal Himself to as the Messiah (John 4:26) and a woman who first witnessed His resurrection (John 20:11–18). Jesus entrusted women with mighty, cosmic-sized divine revelations. And Paul's note here only supports that truth: Women in the early church were included, counterculturally, and elevated to the status of sisters in the Lord.

At this time, hair also had great significance in the culture. Often the prostitutes in the temple shaved their heads, which indicated they were serving pagan gods. But in modern cultures, a shaved head doesn't automatically signal prostitution. There are many unique circumstances not accounted for in Paul's blanket statement about the Corinthians' situation: cancer, alopecia, postpartum hair loss, illness, et cetera. There is no shame to be received from these statements about hair—Paul's words were rooted in a very specific time and situation—and it's also not vain to feel disappointment over hair loss. We know God cares about it.

2. How do we know that (see Luke 12:7)?

Paul's correction in 11:4–6 was about authority and order, and both men and women were being corrected. A head covering at this time in history would signify being under a human authority. Appealing to the order of creation, the men (seemingly both married and single) were meant to pray and prophesy without a head covering to signify that they were under the established authority of Jesus. And wives were meant to pray and prophesy with head coverings to signify that they, too, were under authority.

3. Why does 11:10 say a wife ought to have a symbol of authority on her head?

4. What do you think this phrase means?

Scholars have not reached agreement on what this phrase means. In fact, scholars don't know for sure what *most* of today's passage means. This is one of those passages that's so steeped in cultural significance that it's difficult for us to sort out.

Elements such as the statement in 11:11–12 about how men and women need each other in this order of creation might be less rooted in culture (after all, women still give birth).

But we don't want to scream where Scripture whispers, and we don't want to whisper where Scripture screams. Almost none of this content is addressed anywhere else in the Bible, which leads us to believe Paul was primarily speaking to a cultural situation. It's unwise to build a doctrine or practice around something that only shows up once in Scripture—especially when it remains unclear, and especially when the primary point of this passage *is* stated clearly (11:16): The goal was order, not disagreement.

★ 5. What was the most challenging element of today's passage for you?

★ 6. Was there anything that surprised you?

DAY 5

1 Corinthians 11:17–34

READ 1 CORINTHIANS 11:17–34

Review 11:17–22.

While the Corinthian Christians were coming together to eat, some people were gorging themselves and getting drunk, and others were coming later finding nothing left to eat. This passage reinforces what Paul has been saying in all of this week's study: The problem wasn't about food or drink; it was about self-focus and abusing personal liberties at the expense of one another and the gospel.

Earlier, in 1:10–17, Paul corrected harmful factions and divisions in the church. And here, he returned to the issue, employing one of his classic sarcastic turnabouts. And in 11:19, he basically responded, *"Oh, are there factions? Great—that'll make it easy for me to compliment those with genuine hearts. As for the rest of you . . ."*

"Shall I commend you in this?" may have been in response to a suggestion in their letter to Paul that he should commend them—or perhaps they were simply quite proud of themselves. But it seems Paul had learned that some members were so selfish that they were showing up to scarf down the food and drink. They did this not only at the expense of the communal sense of the event, but they even went so far as to humiliate the poor among them who showed up later—who were very much in need of food—and found no food left.

1. On the gauge below, draw an arrow pointing to Paul's response (see 11:22).

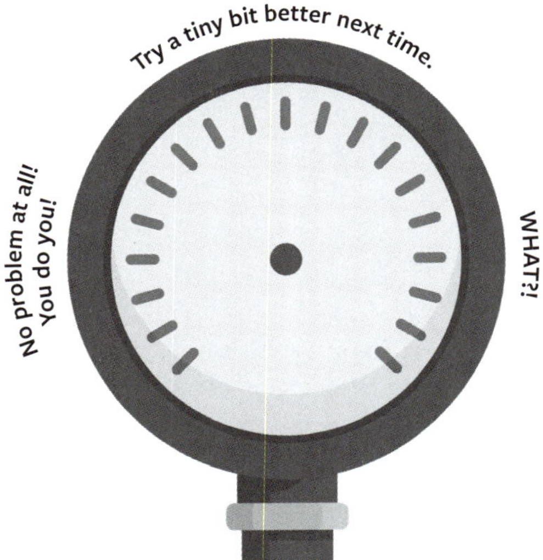

In this Corinthian culture, it was common practice for the upper class to receive more and better food than the lower classes. Paul was extremely disturbed that the church would reflect that inside its gatherings. And this was an area where Paul was saying, *"No, no, no—we don't do it like the world does it."* The early church was the place where freedmen and slaves sat together at meals, where women and men were sisters and brothers in Christ, where the rich and poor "had everything in common" (Acts 4:32)—but the Corinthian church wasn't demonstrating this as God intended. This scenario where the poor among them were showing up to find no food left was deserving of no other response than *"What?!"*

Review 11:23–34.

Paul reminded the Corinthian Christians what the sacrament of the Lord's Table truly is: a remembrance of the saving death of Christ. It's not an event for self-focus and drunkards. Many of them were handling it selfishly, disregarding the good of the whole. However, 11:27 has sometimes resulted in misunderstanding.

2. What do you think 11:27–28 means?

Paul wasn't suggesting that Christians need to get to some state of "worthiness" before participating in Communion. That would be a misrepresentation of what Communion remembers. Communion is the Christian's opportunity to partake in remembrance of Christ's saving work on the cross, which brought us to salvation through faith alone. Our works do not save us; *His* do. We're incapable of making ourselves worthy of Christ's saving act on the cross. Rather, Paul was saying these Corinthians were partaking in Communion with irreverent, unremembering hearts. They were treating the Lord's Table like a Golden Corral.

★ 3. How could 11:30 also be easily misunderstood?

In this very specific Corinthian situation, God apparently disciplined some of their congregation in this way. This passage is *in no way* saying that every weakness, illness, or death is the result of God's discipline. But in 11:31–32, Paul *was* saying they wouldn't need to be disciplined in this way if they would discipline themselves.

4. In your own life or church gatherings, where has satisfying one's own appetite inhibited community and the gospel? Think beyond just food.

★ 5. How could you both discipline yourself in these areas and perhaps even encourage your community to do the same?

Paul ends this section with, "*We'll talk about the rest when I get there.*" We don't know what that follow-up conversation entailed, but we can wonder whether the warning alone prompted the Corinthians to begin examining their hearts. In so many aspects of this week's study, they had been choosing lesser tables—tables of demons, selfishness, cheap lusts, and leftovers from their culture. But Paul encouraged them to leave those microwaved leftovers behind and come to the King's banquet, to which God has invited us. He's where the best RSVP in the universe is, and He's where the joy is!

6. What stood out to you most in this week's study? Why?

7. What did you learn or relearn about God and His character this week?

DAY 6

Corresponding Psalm & Prayer

READ PSALM 16

1. What correlation do you see between Psalm 16 and this week's study?

2. What portions of this psalm stand out to you most?

3. Close by praying this prayer aloud:

Father,

You were with Israel in the wilderness, You were with the Corinthians at their fellowship table, and You are with me now. You've shown us the path of life and You make our joy full. I have no good apart from You.

Lord, I have chosen lesser tables. I've insisted that my struggles are unique, and I've given myself license to sin. I haven't fled from temptation, and so I've given myself an easy path to sin. And even though I haven't bowed to a statue, I have run after idols. So my sorrows have multiplied, and I repent.

Help me remember that the lines have fallen for me in pleasant places—that I have a beautiful inheritance! Help me seek to serve and love—You first, and my neighbors second. May my life reflect Your countercultural kingdom in all things.

Whether I eat, drink, work, sleep, or play, may it be for Your glory. I surrender my life to You, Lord—every moment of my day, each decision I make, I yield my will and way to Your perfect will and way.

I love You too. Amen.

DAY 7

Rest, Catch Up, or Dig Deeper

WEEKLY CHALLENGE

In 1 Corinthians 10:13, God promised that when temptation comes, He'll provide a way of escape. Actively look for the ways God makes good on that promise in your life this week, and *take the escape route!* Create a drawing, a piece of art, or a phone wallpaper that can serve as a reminder when you're tempted. Here are some phrases you might consider incorporating into your art piece or wallpaper:

He is with you!
He will always provide a way of escape!
Take the escape route!

WEEK 5

1 Corinthians 12–14

Scripture to Memorize

Love bears all things, believes all things, hopes all things, endures all things.

1 Corinthians 13:7

DAILY BIBLE READING

Day 1: 1 Corinthians 12:1–11

Day 2: 1 Corinthians 12:12–31

Day 3: 1 Corinthians 13:1–13

Day 4: 1 Corinthians 14:1–25

Day 5: 1 Corinthians 14:26–40

Day 6: Psalm 133

Day 7: Catch-Up Day

Corresponds to Day 336 of *The Bible Recap*.

WEEKLY CHALLENGE

See page 126 for more information.

DAY 1

1 Corinthians 12:1–11

READ 1 CORINTHIANS 12:1–11

Review 12:1–3.

The Corinthians apparently asked questions about spiritual gifts in their letter to Paul, because he opens this section with "Now concerning," as he did in 7:1. Before he answered their questions, he acknowledged the importance of this topic. He wanted the Corinthians to be informed and knowledgeable about these gifts and the way they worked in the church.

★ 1. Mark an X where you are in your understanding of spiritual gifts.

I've studied this topic extensively	I have some opinions	I can list some of the gifts and I think I know what they mean	I've heard of this topic	What?

★ 2. Write what you already know about spiritual gifts (reference Scripture whenever possible). Then write your questions or concerns about them.

Because the church in Corinth was primarily a Gentile church, Paul referred to them as formerly pagan. Their past religious experiences consisted of worshiping idols, but they had begun to worship the triune God—Father, Son, and Holy Spirit—instead. He wanted them to understand how their new relationship with God was distinct from their previous experiences.

3. How did Paul describe the communication style and activity of pagan idols in contrast to the Spirit of God (the Holy Spirit)?

Review 12:4–7.

The Holy Spirit works within the church by empowering God's people through spiritual gifts—many of which the Corinthians were already experiencing. Paul wanted to establish two key points before exploring the specific expressions of spiritual gifts within the church.

4. Fill in the table below.

Verse	What has variety?	What is the same?
12:4		
12:5		
12:6		

Did you notice all three persons of the Trinity mentioned in this section? The nature of the Trinity helps highlight the value God places on unity in the midst of diversity. After all, this is how the triune God operates—His three persons are also distinct and diverse, but united. It shouldn't surprise us that God desires this within His people.

Although the gifts, service, and activity of believers will be unique and distinct in their expressions within the church, the gifts are given by the same God for the building up ("common good") of the one, unified body of Christ—the church (12:7).

Review 12:8–10.

Paul listed nine spiritual gifts in this section; however, this isn't an exhaustive list. Spiritual gifts are mentioned elsewhere in Scripture, and each list varies (see Exodus 31:1–6; Romans 12:6–8; 1 Corinthians 12:9–28; Ephesians 4:11; and 1 Peter 4:9–11). It's possible the gifts he mentioned here were listed because they were the ones most evident in the Corinthian church.

★ 5. **Use Bible study tools to look up each spiritual gift, then briefly describe it in your own words.**

Wisdom ____

____

Knowledge ____

____

Faith ____

____

Healing ____

____

Miracles ____

____

Prophecy ____

____

Distinguishing between spirits ______________________________

____

Tongues ____

____

Interpretation of tongues ______________________________

____

Review 12:11, then reread 12:7.

These two verses highlight the main takeaways Paul wanted to emphasize regarding spiritual gifts. Keep these points in mind the rest of the week as you study and learn more about spiritual gifts.

Point #1: Each believer has a spiritual gift to be used as an expression of the Spirit, as He is always present and active within each believer (see Romans 8:9).

Point #2: God gives the gifts through the Holy Spirit. He is the giver. Believers are the receivers.

Point #3: God distributes the gifts to each believer as He wills. (Note: Paul writes more about this later; we'll see there's nothing wrong with desiring and asking God for spiritual gifts. In fact, Paul encouraged it. But again, God gets to choose the gifts He gives.)

Point #4: Gifts are for the common good. They're for the service, upbuilding, and edification of those within the local church and the global church.

DAY 2

1 Corinthians 12:12–31

 READ 1 CORINTHIANS 12:12–31

Review 12:12–13.

To help the Corinthians understand the experience and expression of spiritual gifts within the church, Paul introduced an image they'd all be familiar with: the human body. Both the body of Christ and the human body exist as one entity made up of different parts.

To further illustrate this point, Paul reminded the Corinthians of their baptism—when they were united with Christ and brought into the *one* family of God. The diversity within the church—Jews, Greeks, slaves, and free people—existed alongside the unity found in the one body of Christ.

1. How many times is the word *one* mentioned in these two verses?

Review 12:14–20.

Paul explained the necessity of diversity among the many members of the human body. It would be foolish for a foot to disqualify itself from the rest of the body because it wasn't a hand. In this same way, Paul hoped the Corinthians would understand the importance each person brought to the church. Each one belonged and was valued.

God created the human body with a diversity of parts so it would function as He intended. In this same way, spiritual gifts are by God's design and the distribution of these gifts is up to Him.

Review 12:21–26.

In the previous section, Paul presented the foot and the ear as thinking too little of their importance in the body. In this metaphor, the eye and the head have a different problem.

2. What do the eye and head say to the other parts of the body? What was Paul's response to this kind of thinking?

Neither viewpoint presented by these body parts—a lack of belonging *or* a lack of need for other parts—aligns with the reality of the human body or the body of Christ. Neither pride nor low self-esteem changes God's stated reality: *All parts are important.*

3. Draw a line connecting the correct phrases.

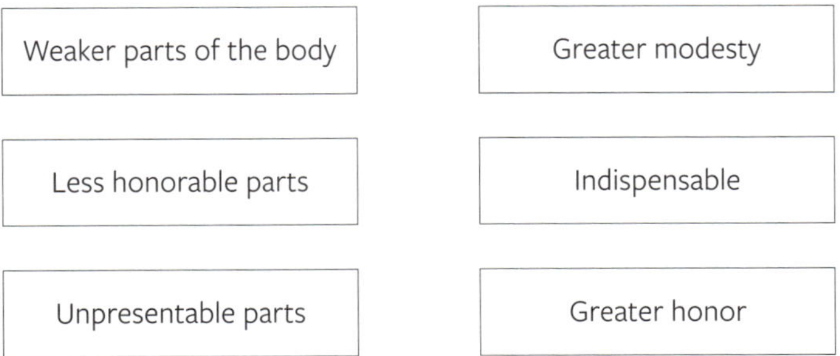

The continuation of Paul's metaphor reminded the Corinthians of the great care humans take to clothe, cover, and honor the parts of the body that need it most. This was true for the weaker, humbler, more needy members of the body of Christ as well.

4. Which of these application points do you think Paul had in mind?

   A. Give honor and assistance to those within the church who are weaker or marginalized.
   B. Care for one another and avoid division.
   C. Recognize that what happens to one member of the church affects the other members.
   D. All of the above.

★ 5. Do you see yourself as belonging within the body of Christ? Explain. Do you look at others within the church as important and necessary members? Explain.

Review 12:27–31.

Paul used another list here, which although not exhaustive, does seem to denote an order of importance (first, second, third, etc.) of the *gift*, but not of the *person*. Apostles, prophets, and teachers were responsible for leadership within the early church. As you've already seen in this letter, the apostles were messengers on behalf of Christ. They had more authority and greater responsibilities than others in the church.

Each person who receives a gift is necessary for the body, and at the same time, some gifts seem to be "higher gifts"—and according to Paul, these two statements aren't contradictory.

Scholars have different opinions as to what Paul meant by "higher gifts." Some think the higher gifts are those of greater importance in his numbered list (e.g., apostles, prophets, and teachers). Others think Paul viewed all gifts besides tongues as higher gifts (you'll learn more about this in 1 Corinthians 14). And others believe it's the gifts considered most useful and beneficial for the current needs of the church.

Paul encouraged the Corinthians to both desire these higher spiritual gifts and walk in the gifts they'd already been given.

★ 6. What spiritual gifts do you desire most? Why? Tell God about your desire.

DAY 3

1 Corinthians 13:1–13

 READ 1 CORINTHIANS 13:1–13

This brief but powerful chapter might feel familiar; perhaps you've heard it read at a wedding. But remember, despite that familiar feeling, Paul's statements about love originated in a particular context—a letter to the divided, spiritually fervent, and often misguided Corinthian church. Paul wrote to encourage them in a better, unified way—the way of love.

Review 13:1–3, then reread 12:31b.

Paul used hyperbole, another common rhetorical device, in these verses to describe the most outrageous events and acts. It's as if he said, *"Imagine the most ecstatic spiritual experience, the wildest acts of faith, and the most selfless acts . . . but no love."*

1. In your own words, how did Paul view these incredible expressions of spiritual gifts when they were devoid of love?

Review 13:4–8a.

2. Fill in the table below.

What love is / does (positive statements) . . .	What love is not / does not do (negative statements) . . .

These descriptions encouraged the Corinthian church to consider their thoughts, motives, and actions as they gathered together. Paul cared about the daily lives of believers *and* how they treated each other at church. Perhaps if they understood and exhibited love in the context of their worship, they could more readily embody love the rest of the week.

Review 13:8b–11.

3. Look up 1 John 4:16 and fill in the blanks.

"So we have come to know and to believe the love that God has for us. God is ________, and whoever abides in love ____________ in ______, and God ____________ in ______."

Paul referred to love as the "more excellent way" because it was connected directly to who God is. Love reveals what God values and what God's heart is like. The spiritual gifts—prophecy, tongues, knowledge—although beneficial for the Corinthians, would eventually end. They're only partial realities of the fullness that will one day be realized in eternity. Love will never end.

Paul's phrase "when the perfect comes" referred to a sense of maturity or completeness, which can only be realized when Jesus returns. In the meantime, growing in maturity was and is an important goal for all

Christians. Paul urged the Corinthians to stop thinking and acting like kids, basically telling them, *"Stop being immature."*

★ 4. Write down areas of maturity and immaturity in your relationship with God. Circle any areas where love is absent.

Maturity	Immaturity

Paul knew the Corinthians were being childish about their spiritual gifts (more on this tomorrow). Before correcting them on this topic, he wanted to give them an anchor point to reframe their thoughts and actions. Love would help instruct, redirect, discipline, and order the expressions of these gifts within their congregation.

Review 13:12.

Many people in the early church assumed that Jesus would return in their lifetime. Paul most likely thought this too—especially early in his ministry. He lived with great anticipation and expectation for the joy of a face-to-face relationship with God. At Christ's return, true maturity and completeness will finally be a reality for all believers.

Review 13:13.

Why is love the only thing that remains? Aren't faith and hope important too? Yes, but one day faith and hope will no longer exist. We wait eagerly for the day when our faith will be made sight (2 Corinthians 5:7) and our hope will be fulfilled (Romans 8:24–25). Someday we won't need faith and hope anymore, but love will outlast both! Until that day, we walk by faith, full of hope and empowered by love.

★ 5. How do the three things Paul listed in 13:13 help, encourage, and strengthen you as you wait for Christ's return?

DAY 4

1 Corinthians 14:1–25

 READ 1 CORINTHIANS 14:1–25

Depending on your church background or past experiences, this passage might bring up feelings of confusion, excitement, discomfort, or some combination of those. To bring as much clarity to Paul's words as possible, let's get on the same page about a few things.

First, Paul had a lot to say about the gift of tongues, but nowhere in this text did he identify tongues as evidence of salvation; the topic of salvation isn't even mentioned in this text. Tongues are *one* of the many spiritual gifts, which are given by God to believers. They are not *the* gift that proves you are saved or have the Holy Spirit dwelling within you. All Christians have the presence of the Holy Spirit with them at all times, regardless of whether they speak in tongues (Romans 8:9; John 14:17). Paul even clarified this earlier in 1 Corinthians 3:16.

Second, because God chooses to give certain gifts to certain believers and doesn't give every gift to every believer, not everyone should expect to receive the gift of tongues.

Third, Paul affirmed the goodness of the spiritual gifts—after all, they are from God (James 1:17)! Paul encouraged Christians to desire the gifts, and as you'll see, there's nothing wrong with asking God for specific gifts. The gifts are expressions of the Holy Spirit at work in believers; they should never be used to manipulate or discourage—this would ignore Paul's appeal to the greater way of love.

Feeling good? Okay, let's dig in.

Review 14:1.

Paul had a lot to say about the Corinthians' misguided expressions of the gift of tongues within their worship gatherings. But before he corrected them, he gave two instructions that demonstrate his heart and hope for this church.

1. What two commands did Paul give in 14:1?

Review 14:2–5.

The heading for this passage in your Bible might be something like "Prophecy and Tongues," like it is in the ESV. Paul contrasted these two gifts because the improper use of tongues was leading to confusion and disorder during the Corinthians' church services.

The Greek word used for "tongues" in 14:2 remains the same throughout this entire section. It simply means "speech" or "language." There are two main views for how to understand what this language might be.

View A: tongues are human languages	View B: tongues are heavenly languages
"Tongues" refers to a human language (e.g., Greek, Spanish) that was either known or unknown by the speaker. Paul was a polyglot (someone who spoke many different languages), so when he "spoke in tongues," he would have been speaking in any one of a variety of languages, including Greek, Aramaic, Hebrew, et cetera. Depending on the context, the language might sound foreign to those around him (depending on whether they knew the language or the Spirit gave them understanding), but it was a known, human language.	"Tongues" refers to speaking a heavenly or spiritual language. This language is known only by God; it is not a human language.

Keep these two views in mind going forward.

2. In 14:3–4, what are the benefits of prophecy? In 14:5, what was Paul's goal for the expression of spiritual gifts within the church?

Review 14:6–12.

It might seem like Paul held a negative view of the gift of tongues, but he didn't. In fact, he spoke in tongues (14:18) and affirmed the gift's place within the church (14:27–28). What he was *not* thrilled about was the preference those speaking in tongues were placing on themselves rather than on those around them.

Whether you align more with view A or view B above, Paul's point remained the same: Without an interpreter (someone who understood both languages), people would be confused and the church wouldn't benefit or be built up.

Review 14:13–19.

3. In 14:13, what did Paul instruct the person speaking in tongues to pray for?

Paul referenced the interpretation of tongues in 12:10. Those who believe view A would see this interpretation as someone who spoke the main language of the congregation (e.g., Spanish) and the tongue language (e.g., French) translating what was said in French into Spanish so everyone could understand. View B would see this interpretation as someone being able to translate the heavenly language into the appropriate human language. In both examples, the person speaking the tongue could also be their own translator.

Paul cared about the entire congregation's experience and mutual edification in worship. So he encouraged those speaking in tongues to praise God with their mind, basically saying, *"Praise God in a way that the person sitting next to you can say 'Amen' to."* For Paul, five words that everyone understood were better than ten thousand words that no one understood.

Review 14:20–22.

Back in 13:11, Paul encouraged the Corinthians to grow in their maturity. Here, he reiterated the necessity of mature thinking regarding the expressions of their spiritual gifts. He referenced Isaiah 28:11–12, in which God planned to speak to His people through a foreign language—that of the invading Assyrian armies. This was going to be a sign to the Jewish people. Paul's reference to tongues as a sign to unbelievers in the Corinthian church might mean that the very act of God speaking through the Corinthians was a sign to unbelievers, but as Paul goes on to say, it might not be all that helpful for them.

Review 14:23–25.

4. According to these verses how would the unbelieving church visitor respond to people speaking in tongues in church? How would that same visitor respond to people prophesying?

When the Corinthians gathered for worship, Paul wanted everyone in the congregation to be built up. He also hoped God's presence would be undeniable—for their benefit and also for the possible salvation of any unbelievers who visited the church that day.

★ 5. After studying this passage, which view makes more sense to you, view A or B? Explain.

★ 6. Write down one or two new things you learned from today's lesson and one or two questions you want to study more.

DAY 5

1 Corinthians 14:26–40

 **READ 1 CORINTHIANS 14:26–40**

Paul began correcting and instructing the Corinthians about their worship gatherings way back in 1 Corinthians 11. And here you see his concluding thoughts on proper conduct and practices for this misguided church. As you study this section, keep in mind that Paul wrote this letter to the Corinthians in their unique cultural context. This will help as you consider some of the more confusing or difficult statements he made.

Review 14:26.

1. List the four things the Corinthians were to include in their gathering times. Use Bible study tools to look up the definitions and briefly define them in your own words. Write down Paul's goal for these activities.

A.

B.

C.

D.

Goal:

2. Read Colossians 3:16 and Acts 2:42. Write down the things that weren't mentioned in Paul's list to the Corinthians.

Colossians 3:16

Acts 2:42

There's no place in the New Testament where the content or activities of church gatherings were clearly defined. However, there was agreement as to the general idea of what should take place.

★ 3. Consider your church's worship gatherings. What similarities do they have with these New Testament examples? What differences? Is there anything you wish your church would include?

Review 14:27–33a.

As you read in Day 4, Paul had some correcting to do because of the way the Corinthians expressed their spiritual gifts during worship. Here, he gave specific instructions for how to speak in tongues and prophesy. Two or three people could speak in tongues (as long as there was interpretation), and two or three people could prophesy (but others must evaluate the truthfulness of what was said). His main concern, however, was that the Corinthians took turns speaking.

Think back to 13:4–5 when he instructed the Corinthians in the way of love. He used words like *patient*, *kind*, *not arrogant*, *not rude*, *not insisting on their own way*. Most likely, he had their disorderly gatherings in mind. The Corinthians' passionate spiritual expressions were leading to chaos because they kept interrupting each other. Paul reminded them that God is a God of peace. He brings peace—not confusion—to their worship.

Review 14:33b–35.

If this section felt like a hard left turn, you're not alone. At first glance it can be difficult to understand exactly what Paul meant by these words. (Note: It also might be difficult after many glances; scholars and theologians don't often agree on what Paul meant either.)

Let's start with what Paul had already taught. First, it's clear that he expected women to pray and prophesy in church (11:5, 13). So he can't mean women should never speak in church. Second, it's clear that spiritual gifts were for every believer and were to be used in the worship gathering. Both men and women have gifts of teaching, prophecy, knowledge, tongues—all of which involve speaking. Third, as Manfred Brauch points out in his book *Hard Sayings of Paul*, Paul used the same Greek word *sigaō* (meaning "remain silent") in his instructions to those of both genders who spoke in tongues and prophesied (14:28, 30). This is the same word he used in 14:34.[1]

In the context of the Corinthian church, there were also some cultural considerations to bear in mind. Women were generally uneducated, and in Greek culture specifically, they were discouraged from talking in public.[2] Paul reversed these cultural norms, encouraging women to pray and prophesy (i.e., speak in public). But perhaps some women were taking their newfound freedom a bit too far and disrupting the service because of it.

The seating situation may have also added to the problem. Men and women were most likely seated separately, which was the custom in Jewish synagogues. The Corinthians might have adopted this practice as well. So if a woman was confused about something and wanted to ask her husband, she couldn't subtly whisper to him—he was all the way across the room.[3]

Paul wanted the chaos in the Corinthian church to stop. He called on those who spoke in tongues, those who prophesied, and women who were speaking out of turn (perhaps in a disrespectful, dishonoring, or chaos-causing way) to remain silent so that others could also have their time to share.

Studying this passage provides a helpful reminder to avoid building doctrine from a few verses. Though there will probably be a long line to talk to Paul in eternity and thank him for all he contributed to our faith, hopefully he'll be fielding questions too. Between head coverings, "because of the angels" (11:10), and this passage, he might be busy for a while.

★ 4. What do you think Paul meant in these verses? What parts do you still have questions about?

Review 14:36–40.

Paul's tone might sound familiar here. The Corinthians' pride caused them to disregard his authority in a number of matters; they assumed they knew best. Once again, he reminded them that the things he'd instructed them on are from the Lord. If they considered themselves to be spiritually elite, they might want to shape up.

Paul's desire was for God to be glorified and worshiped when the church came together. The gathering was not for their entertainment but for their edification—so everyone could be built up in Christ. Glorifying God together brings a unity and a peace we can't find elsewhere. He's where the peace is, and He's where the joy is!

5. What stood out to you most in this week's study? Why?

6. What did you learn or relearn about God and His character this week?

DAY 6

Corresponding Psalm & Prayer

READ PSALM 133

1. What correlation do you see between Psalm 133 and this week's study?

2. What portions of this psalm stand out to you most?

3. Close by praying this prayer aloud:

Father,

You created diversity and You created unity. Both are beautiful and necessary for flourishing! You're the giver of all good gifts, including the unique abilities You've given each of us. I praise You for being endlessly creative and infinitely attentive.

But instead of dwelling in unity, I've sown division. I've argued over secondary issues, and I've discounted my brothers and sisters because of minor disagreements. I've screamed where Scripture whispers, and I've confused, misled, or hurt others in the process. I've been a noisy gong and a clanging cymbal. I've torn down instead of building up. Forgive me.

Make me patient and kind, bearing all things, hoping all things, and believing all things. Let Your church dwell in unity. Let us be like precious anointing oil, or the morning-fresh dew on Zion's mountains. Give us Your blessing—life full and forever—complete in You.

Lead me in the more excellent way. I surrender my life to You, Lord—every moment of my day, each decision I make, I yield my will and way to Your perfect will and way.

I love You too. Amen.

DAY 7

Rest, Catch Up, or Dig Deeper

WEEKLY CHALLENGE

Under Day 1's second prompt, you listed out your concerns and questions about spiritual gifts. Look back to see if any of those concerns or questions remain after completing this week's study. If so, choose one to two items and research them using Bible study tools.

WEEK 6

1 Corinthians 15–16

Scripture to Memorize

Love never ends. As for prophecies, they will pass away; as for tongues, they will cease; as for knowledge, it will pass away.

1 Corinthians 13:8

DAILY BIBLE READING

Day 1: 1 Corinthians 15:1–11

Day 2: 1 Corinthians 15:12–34

Day 3: 1 Corinthians 15:35–58

Day 4: 1 Corinthians 16:1–11

Day 5: 1 Corinthians 16:12–24

Day 6: Psalm 110

Day 7: Catch-Up Day

Corresponds to Day 337 of *The Bible Recap*.

WEEKLY CHALLENGE

See page 151 for more information.

DAY 1

1 Corinthians 15:1–11

READ 1 CORINTHIANS 15:1–11

Review 15:1–2.

The Corinthians likely hadn't asked Paul specific questions about the gospel (or the resurrection), but some misguided beliefs were circling within the church about these topics. Paul seized the opportunity to ensure the Corinthians understood the full picture of the good news of Jesus Christ.

1. Write down the phrases from 15:1–2 that correlate with the past, present, and future reality of the Corinthians' salvation.

Past	Present	Present-Future

Paul preached the gospel to the Corinthians during his second missionary journey (Acts 18:1–11). He remembered their conversions and knew they were sincere in their faith. Therefore, he was confident their salvation was secure and wanted them to be confident too.

There are a variety of reasons Christians might struggle to believe their salvation is secure—such as ongoing sin issues, questions about the validity of a conversion experience, and general doubts about God. It's important to remember in those seasons that, just like the Corinthians, you *are being* saved. You have put your faith in the finished work of Jesus—not your own works. And as Paul wrote elsewhere, "He who began a good work in you will bring it to completion at the day of Jesus Christ" (Philippians 1:6). He began it, He is continuing it, and He will complete it. *He does the doing.*

★ 2. Have you struggled to believe your salvation is secure? Or has someone you know experienced this struggle?

3. Look up the verses below and take note of anything helpful that stands out to you.

John 5:24

1 John 5:11–13

Review 15:3–4.

The gospel is the most important message anyone could ever share or receive. Paul knew this and lived his whole life according to this truth. He wanted the Corinthians to understand this too.

Even though you might know the importance of the gospel, you may have found it hard to know how to share it. Paul helped us with that by his clear and concise definition.

4. Using 15:3–4 fill in the table below.

What is the gospel?	What evidence listed (if any) supports that detail?

Review 15:5–7.

5. In the left column, circle the eyewitnesses who saw Jesus after He was raised from the dead. (We'll use the right column in a moment.)

Cephas	__________________________
The twelve	__________________________
Samuel	
Five hundred brothers at one time	__________________________
Moses	__________________________
Isaiah	__________________________
James	
All the apostles	
Rahab	

Unfortunately, the women who were the first eyewitnesses to the resurrected Jesus (Mary Magdalene, Joanna, Mary the mother of Jesus, Mary the mother of James, and Salome in John 20:1–18; Luke 23:54–24:12; Mark 15:40–16:8; Matthew 28:5–8) didn't make the list. This could've been due to the low credibility women had at that time—they weren't accepted as witnesses.[1]

It's not that Paul wanted to exclude them, but his goal was to provide *irrefutable evidence* to the doubters in the Corinthian church, verifying that Jesus most certainly rose from the dead. To avoid any possible denial of these eyewitnesses, Paul listed sources who couldn't possibly be discredited. Surely he wouldn't mind if you added those five women's names to the list now, though, so go ahead and do that above.

Review 15:8–11.

Paul presented himself as the final eyewitness for the Corinthians' consideration. He called himself "one untimely born" and "the least of the apostles, unworthy to be called an apostle," because he wasn't a disciple during Jesus's ministry, nor was he an early (or eager) convert. Paul originally wanted nothing to do with Jesus and instead imprisoned, persecuted, and murdered Christians. But Jesus met him on the road to Damascus and made Paul an eyewitness! Now you can add his name to the list above too.

The grace of God brought Paul into God's family. And the grace of God empowered him to work hard, alongside the other apostles and eyewitnesses, to spread the good news of Jesus's life, death, and resurrection.

This was the truth of what the Corinthians first believed, and they needed to reorient their lives around this message: Jesus is alive!

★ 6. Write down one to two ways you've seen God's grace in your life this week. Write a prayer of thanksgiving for this grace.

7. How does today's passage help you feel more confident in sharing the gospel? Explain.

DAY 2

1 Corinthians 15:12–34

READ 1 CORINTHIANS 15:12–34

Review 15:12–19.

Resurrection was a commonly held Jewish belief, but the Sadducees, a Jewish sect, denied the resurrection of the dead. Both Jesus and Paul disputed this topic with them (Mark 12:18–27; Acts 23:6–10). Greek culture viewed the afterlife as a time when disembodied spirits were finally free from their horrible, fleshly existence. Philosophers scoffed at the idea of a bodily resurrection, as we see in Acts 17, when Paul spoke in Athens (Acts 17:16–34).[1]

Paul had dealt with these views *outside* of the church, but here he was having to defend the resurrection to people who should've known better (15:3–4). You can sense Paul's exasperation as he basically said, "*How can you act like there's no resurrection? Remember when I shared the gospel with you? And what about all those eyewitnesses—including me?!*"

1. Fill in the flowchart below with the six main problems Paul exposed in the Corinthians' logic.

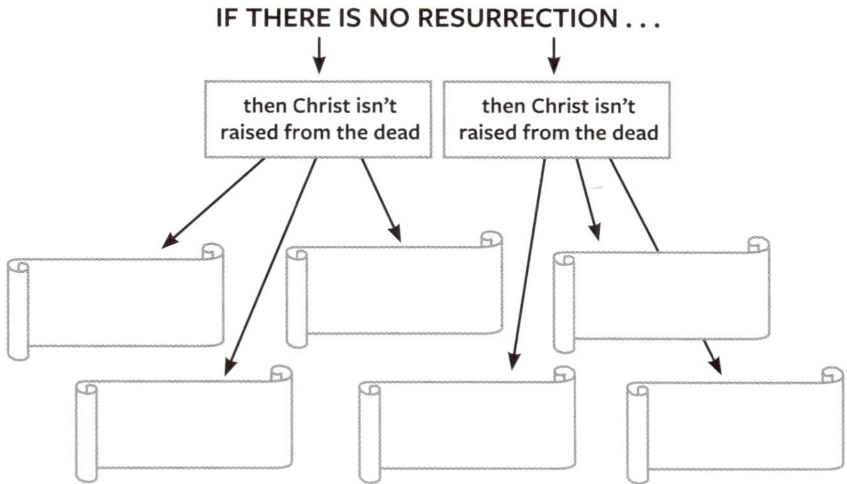

Denying the resurrection was a big deal! First, it contradicted the gospel message, and second, there was still that pesky sin problem to deal with—how would their sins be defeated otherwise?! For Paul, there was either hope in Christ—which led to a changed way of thinking and living—or there wasn't. The Corinthians wanted to deny the resurrection but still call themselves Christians. But that lifestyle was one to be pitied.

Review 15:20.

Even though this was where the Corinthians' belief logically led them, they didn't have to stay there. The joyful, hopeful truth was that Christ *had* been raised from the dead, and they could expect to be raised to new life too.

In Greek culture, firstfruits referred to an admission fee, like how we pay to enter a museum or cultural site today.[2] For the Jews, this term referred back to Leviticus and a harvest celebration where the people brought their first crops as an offering to God in anticipation of greater bounty (Leviticus 23:9–14). Jesus's resurrection solidified both of these things for believers—our entrance fee has been paid *and* the bounty of our future resurrection is secure.

★ 2. Does Jesus's resurrection give you hope and confidence for your future resurrection and the life to come? Explain.

Review 15:21–22.

3. Fill in the chart below with Paul's logic.

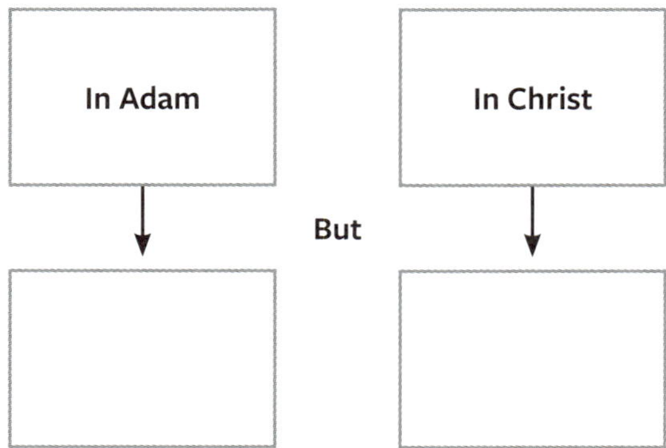

Review 15:23–28.

Paul referenced Christ's return here, at which time believers—and unbelievers—will be resurrected. The Greek word translated "the end" (*telos*) denotes a conclusion, final act, or fulfillment. Christ's return is the moment all history has been moving toward.

4. This passage is steeped in kingdom language. Write down all the words or phrases you see that relate to the kingdom.

God is sovereign over all things, but it might not always feel that way—sin, brokenness, death, and pain can be all too real for us at times. But when Christ returns, we can rest assured He will destroy death and deal with sin, and all things will finally be in submission to Him.

Christ will reign, and just as He humbly did the will of His Father during His earthly ministry (John 6:38), He will then present the kingdom to His Father. God's glorious rule and reign will at last be realized over all the earth.

Review 15:29.

Baptism "on behalf of the dead" was most likely a custom the Corinthians were familiar with—and unfortunately seemed to be practicing in their church. Some scholars think this meant the Corinthians were being baptized on behalf of unbelieving friends or relatives who had passed away. Others believe the practice was done on behalf of Christians who had died prior to being baptized.

Paul's main point wasn't about the practice itself but about the inconsistency in the Corinthians' beliefs, which led to hypocrisy in the way they lived. After all, if there was no resurrection of the dead, why were they worried about the afterlife of those dead people?

★ 5. Do you see any inconsistencies in what you say you believe and how you live? Are there areas where you need to course-correct? Explain.

Review 15:30–34.

This was the final logical step for Paul in his reasonable argument. If there is no resurrection, why does it matter how we live? Paul experienced all kinds of persecution and danger throughout his life, but if he thought the same way the Corinthians did, none of his struggles would be worth it—he might as well have just lived it up while he could. But Paul knew that their way of thinking was pure deception.

Paul was adamant that the Corinthians "wake up from [their] drunken stupor" and repent. Their foolishness in allowing culture to dictate their views on the resurrection—and in denying the very truth of the gospel—was appalling. He essentially said, "*You should be ashamed of yourselves!*"

★ 6. Based on what you've learned so far, why do you think Paul reacted so strongly to this misguided belief within the Corinthian church?

7. Ask God to reveal any misguided beliefs you might have. Write a prayer below.

DAY 3

1 Corinthians 15:35–58

READ 1 CORINTHIANS 15:35–58

Review 15:35–36.

The Corinthians may have been wondering, *How exactly is God going to put our bodies back together? And do we want Him to?* Paul had to address the practical implications of how God resurrects bodies—does He just resuscitate their dead, decaying corpses or does something transformative and supernatural occur?

He also needed to help the Corinthians understand that their bodies were good—they should *want* them resurrected. Some in the church had clearly been swayed by Greek culture. Influenced by Plato, the Greeks were dualistic, labeling the spirit as good and the body as bad.[1] But the biblical view of creation and resurrection affirms the goodness of both spirit and body!

★ 1. Describe the tone Paul used in 15:36. Why do you think he reacted this way?

Review 15:37–42.

2. Fill in the table below with the three "body" examples. Make note of what Paul says about each one.

Kernel/Seed	Earthly Bodies	Heavenly Bodies
• Seeds are sown (die) •	• Not all flesh is the same • •	• One glory of the sun • •

3. In the table above, write 15:42a underneath Paul's examples.

Paul applied these concepts to the future resurrected human body. Like the seed, the body dies, but it will be "raised imperishable." The weakness and dishonor in earthly bodies will be replaced with glory and power. A natural body will become a spiritual body.

Review 15:43–49.

4. Write Paul's descriptions of Adam and Jesus (the last Adam) below.

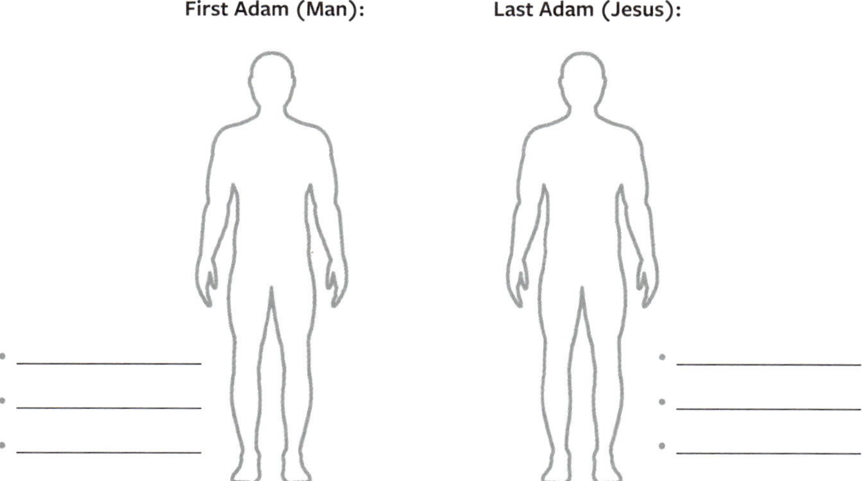

Humanity has always borne the image of God (Genesis 1:26–27). Since Adam, we have also borne the image of the man of dust (Genesis 3:19). However, because of Jesus's resurrection we can look forward to a time when we will bear the image of the heavenly man in our own resurrected bodies.

Review 15:50–53.

Paul was basically saying, "*You're going to want these resurrected bodies—they're the only way to inherit the kingdom.*"

5. **Use a Greek lexicon and a Bible dictionary to look up the word *mystery* (15:51).** Write the definition in your own words.

Not everyone will experience death (some people will still be alive when Christ returns) but everyone will be changed. Paul said this will take place "in a moment." The dead will be raised to life and those still alive will put on immortality—all in "the twinkling of an eye."

Review 15:54–57.

Finally, Paul assured his readers that death would be conquered at Christ's future return. For some of you, death might feel like a distant reality—the thought rarely entering your mind. For others it might feel uncomfortably close with the arrival of another birthday, a recent diagnosis, or the death of a loved one. Remember this: Although we feel the sting of death now, victory over death is ours through Christ Jesus. There will be a time when death will be swallowed up, never to torment or grieve again. "Thanks be to God" for that victory!

★ 6. Think back over Days 1 and 2 and what you've learned so far today. Has this study changed how you think about death or resurrection? Has it brought up further questions for consideration? Write them down below.

Review 15:58.

Paul ended this passage with a term of endearment for the Corinthians. Yes, he might have called them foolish and scolded them severely, but they were his beloved brothers and sisters. They needed a major adjustment in their thinking, for their own benefit and for the sake of their work and witness for the Lord.

7. List the three charges Paul gave the Corinthians and his note of encouragement.

Charge A:

Charge B:

Charge C:

Encouragement:

DAY 4

1 Corinthians 16:1–11

READ 1 CORINTHIANS 16:1–11

Review 16:1.

Once again, Paul referenced the Corinthians' letter to him ("Now concerning . . ."). The church had probably asked him for instructions about the financial collection requested for "the saints."

We know from other passages that this financial gift was for the believers in Jerusalem who might have been experiencing hardship due to a famine (Acts 11:27–30, 24:17; Romans 15:26; 2 Corinthians 8:13, 9:9–12). The Greek word for "collection" (*logia*) means "an extra collection." This would've been above and beyond the Corinthians' normal giving in the context of their church body.[1]

1. What other churches were involved in this collection?

   A. Galatia

   B. Macedonia

   C. Ephesus

   D. None. The Corinthians were the only church expected to give.

2. These churches in Galatia most likely included the locations of Pisidian Antioch, Iconium, Lystra, and Derbe. Draw a church building on each of these locations on the map.

Review 16:2–4.

3. Fill in the table below.

Instructions and Information about the Collection

When to collect:	
Who gives:	
What to do:	
Goal:	
Who carries it:	
Where it goes:	

The phrase "as he may prosper" likely meant Paul didn't expect everyone in the church to give the same amount, but he expected everyone to participate. It was up to the individual or family to consider their financial situation and give what they could.

The collection for the Jerusalem church—and the instructions surrounding it—were given to the Corinthians in their specific context. These aren't necessarily hard and fast "rules for giving" for us today; and this scenario is different from tithing. However, as we encounter these instances in Scripture it can be helpful to consider what principles and application points God might have for our lives.

★ 4. What principles for giving do you follow? How might Paul's instructions to the Corinthians guide your practices or change your perspective on giving?

Review 16:5–9.

5. On the map below today's second prompt, draw a dotted line to mark Paul's travel plans. (*Hint #1:* Paul mentioned his location in 16:8. *Hint #2:* Be sure to include the cities of Philippi, Thessalonica, and Berea in Paul's travels through Macedonia. He most likely would have stopped to visit these churches on his way.)

Paul hoped to spend some quality time with his friends in Corinth, and he also presented his plans open-handedly before the Lord. But he wasn't quite ready to leave Ephesus—there was still important work to do.

Paul faced some form of opposition during his time in Ephesus, but this didn't stop him from recognizing the ministry opportunities available. These two things weren't mutually exclusive. There were certainly times in Paul's travels when adversaries caused him to leave—sometimes by his own choice and other times for fear of his life. But there were other times when Paul endured conflicts because he knew there were incredible opportunities for effective kingdom work. He made his decisions based on the prompting of the Spirit and the circumstances God allowed (1 Corinthians 16:7; Acts 16:6–10).

★ 6. How do you view opposition in your life or ministry? Have you ever experienced great opportunities in the midst of difficulties? Explain.

Review 16:10–11.

7. In the speech bubbles write how Paul expected the Corinthians to treat Timothy. Write why he expected this treatment in the box.

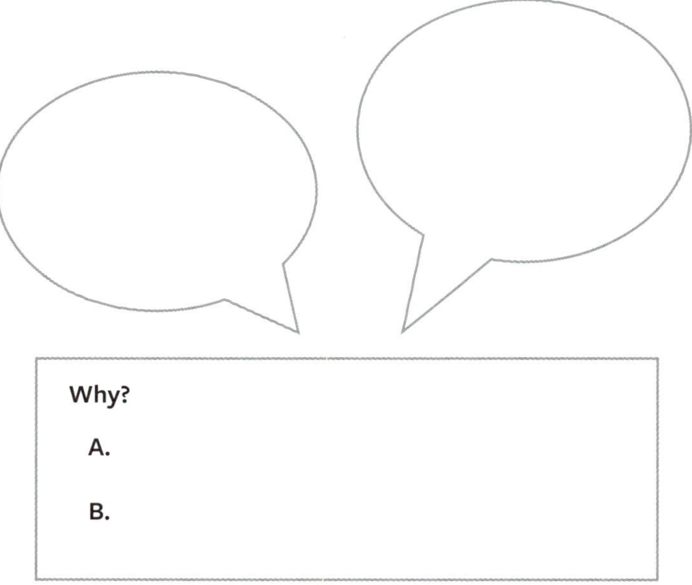

Perhaps Timothy was a little wary about visiting the Corinthians. Or perhaps Paul just wanted to protect his friend and coworker from a potentially uncomfortable situation. Either way, Paul reminded the Corinthians that when Timothy returned to him, he was expecting a good report.

DAY 5

1 Corinthians 16:12–24

 **READ 1 CORINTHIANS 16:12–24**

Review 16:12.

Remember those people in 3:4 who essentially started an Apollos fan club? Apparently they were hoping he would visit them again. Despite encouragement from Paul, Apollos decided against a trip to Corinth. (They'll just have to wait until next time to get Apollos's autograph.)

You may be inclined to picture Paul as the head church planter and leader at this time, perhaps because of all the stories we know from Acts. This might also lead you to think all the other church leaders had to do whatever he said. But that's not what we see here. Paul "urged" Apollos to visit, but Apollos—an apostle and leader in his own right—didn't want to go. In fact, Paul recorded, "It was not at all his will to come now." While we don't know the deeper reason behind the no, it's possible Apollos felt it was God's will to hold off on the visit.

Review 16:13–14.

★ 1. Write down the five commands in 16:13–14. Consider Paul's correction and instruction throughout 1 Corinthians. Why do you think Paul gave these specific reminders to close out his letter? Write your answers beside each command.

A.

B.

C.

D.

E.

Review 16:15–18.

We first heard about Stephanas in 1:16, where we learned he was baptized by Paul. Here, he's mentioned as one of the first converts in the region of Achaia (where Corinth is located). Most likely, he was also one of the people who delivered the Corinthians' letter to Paul, along with Fortunatus and Achaicus.

2. How did Paul ask the Corinthians to treat these men? Put a check mark next to the right answer(s).

- ☐ Be subject (submissive) to them.
- ☐ Give recognition to them.
- ☐ Ignore them.
- ☐ Ask them when Apollos is coming.

★ 3. How did Paul describe Stephanas, Fortunatus, and Achaicus and their actions toward him? Based on what you've learned in 1 Corinthians, why should these things garner respect and submission within the church?

Review 16:19–20.

"The churches of Asia" would have included Ephesus, where Paul wrote this letter from, and likely believers from Colossae, Laodicea, and Hierapolis as well. Flip back to the map in Day 4, and mark these churches.

Aquila and Prisca were familiar names to the Corinthian church. This married couple had previously lived in Corinth, and when Paul first arrived, he worked closely with them making tents (Acts 18:1–3). When Paul wrote this letter they were all in Ephesus together.

Review 16:21–24.

Paul usually had a scribe who wrote his letters—Sosthenes may have written this one (1:1), but scholars are divided on that. Regardless of who it was, Paul grabbed the quill from his scribe and finished off this letter with one final word of warning and hope in his own handwriting.

4. Fill in the blanks in 16:22 below.

"If __________ has no ________ for the ________, let him be ______________.

Our ________, come!"

You may be familiar with the Aramaic word *maranatha*, which means "our Lord, come." Instead of translating the word into Greek here, Paul kept it in Aramaic. This saying was most likely widely known and used within the early church.[1] The Corinthians may have said it in their worship services.

Paul ends many of his letters by recognizing a brother or sister and with a request for God's grace to be with his readers. Here, he also included a reminder of his love for the Corinthians. They've been through a lot together, and there's more to come. (We're looking at you, 2 Corinthians.) But what encouraged Paul and sustained his devotion to the Corinthians were the hope of Christ's return, the love given to believers through Christ, and the gift of grace found in Jesus every day. He's where the joy is!

5. What stood out to you most in this week's study? Why?

6. What did you learn or relearn about God and His character this week?

DAY 6

Corresponding Psalm & Prayer

READ PSALM 110

1. What correlation do you see between Psalm 110 and this week's study?

2. What portions of this psalm stand out to you most?

3. Close by praying this prayer aloud:

Father,

Thank You for sending Your Son, who lived and died and rose again! You are sovereign over this entire fallen world. You judge righteously, rule blamelessly, and bless generously. Like David wrote, You put Your enemies under Your feet. And like Paul taught, when Your Son returns, sorrow, death, and sin will be no more!

My own sin has led to sorrow and death. Maybe I haven't denied You with my words, but I haven't proclaimed You either. Maybe I haven't doubted Your resurrection, but at times, I've lived like it didn't happen. Like the Corinthians, I've walked around in a stupor, ignoring Your commands or clinging to misguided beliefs about You. I repent.

Let me always remember Your Son. Let His life, death, and resurrection impact every moment of every day. Make me an obedient servant. Make me a generous and joyful giver. Make me bold in sharing the good news about You. And let all I do be done in love.

Maranatha—come quickly, Lord Jesus. Conquer sorrow, death, and sin. Redeem this body to live in Your eternal kingdom. And in the meantime, I surrender my life to You, Lord—every moment of my day, each decision I make, I yield my will and way to Your perfect will and way.

I love You too. Amen.

DAY 7

Rest, Catch Up, or Dig Deeper

WEEKLY CHALLENGE

On Day 1, in question 4, you wrote down Paul's definition of the gospel. In question 7 you reflected on how your study helped increase your confidence in sharing the gospel. Put all of this into practice this week by 1) praying for an opportunity and 2) sharing the good news with someone God brings across your path this week!

INTRODUCTION TO 2 CORINTHIANS

Though we've already had an official introduction, here's a quick refresher before starting 2 Corinthians. First Corinthians was largely about Paul forcefully calling the Corinthian Christians to a higher standard. He wasn't playing around and likely stepped on some sensitive toes!

Roughly a year passed between these two letters, and in that time, Paul probably visited them and perhaps even wrote 1.5 Corinthians.

From Philippi, Paul wrote 2 Corinthians with a strong tone of reconciliation between the Corinthian church and his ministry. We see this in 2 Corinthians 1, where he introduces "we" language that was either referring to just himself and Timothy or all the apostles collectively.

Paul had seen many of the believers soften their hearts and move toward repentance. He wasn't shy about pointing out how he was encouraged by their changed lives! In this letter, you'll find Paul's sarcasm to be limited to a deep sense of protection for them instead of firm rebuke. He desperately wanted them to continue down this new path and keep taking strides in their maturity.

As you begin studying 2 Corinthians, look for the differences from Paul's perspective in 1 Corinthians, and be encouraged by the growth he noted in the Corinthian church!

WEEK 7

2 Corinthians 1–4

Scripture to Memorize

For we know in part and
we prophesy in part, but
when the perfect comes,
the partial will pass away.

1 Corinthians 13:9–10

DAILY BIBLE READING

Day 1: 2 Corinthians 1:1–11

Day 2: 2 Corinthians 1:12–24

Day 3: 2 Corinthians 2:1–17

Day 4: 2 Corinthians 3:1–18

Day 5: 2 Corinthians 4:1–18

Day 6: Psalm 30

Day 7: Catch-Up Day

Corresponds to Day 338 of *The Bible Recap*.

WEEKLY CHALLENGE

See page 178 for more information.

DAY 1

2 Corinthians 1:1–11

In the greeting of 1 Corinthians, we studied Paul's position and authority as an apostle. Let's review, using what he wrote here in the greeting of 2 Corinthians.

Review 1:1–2.

1. Address the envelope below.

Sender 1
Name:
Title:
Authority:

Sender 2
Name:
Title:

Recipients:
With:

In his previous letter, Paul told the church at Corinth that they were "called to be saints" (1 Corinthians 1:2), reminding them that God had initiated this relationship with them. His letter of admonition had prompted them to repent. And by the grace of God, their hearts were turned back toward Him. Here again, Paul opens by affirming them as "saints" (1:1). Their calling continues to be proven as they walk in repentance.

As you study, take note of the tone shift from his last letter. While the church at Corinth desperately needed admonishment when Paul wrote 1 Corinthians, now it was time for reconciliation.

In the first century, the usual Greek greeting was *charein*. The Greek word for *grace*, *charis*, was closely related. The usual Hebrew greeting at the time was *peace*, or *salom* ("*shalom*"). So in many of his letters, polyglot Paul cleverly combined the two, making sure all his readers felt included and helping them see God's heart for a multicultural kingdom.[1] "Grace to you," he wrote, "and peace."

Review 1:3–7.

As he introduced the first theme of his letter—comfort in affliction—Paul began with praise. "The God and Father of our Lord Jesus Christ" described God the Father's relationship with Jesus, and "the Father of mercies and God of all comfort" described God the Son's relationship with His people.[2] And though He's not named directly in this verse, God the Spirit is there, too, as the one who comforts us in our affliction (John 14:16).

2. **Using a Greek lexicon, look up the words below and write what you learn.**

Affliction (1:4)—*thlipsis*	Comfort (1:4)—*paraklēsis*

By doing Christ's will, Paul shared in His sufferings (Acts 9:1–19). From the time of his conversion, Paul was no stranger to affliction. By this point in his ministry, Paul had been plotted against, run out of town, arrested, imprisoned, and even stoned. Paul's opponents said that all his afflictions proved he *wasn't* serving God. But make no mistake: Affliction is of the world. Comfort is from God. Paul pointed out to the Corinthians that God had a plan even for the affliction their enemies enacted, and the same is true today: When we are afflicted, we have access to God's comfort. And when we receive comfort, we're able to comfort others in their affliction. So when God gives comfort, it's not just for us, but for others as well.

★ 3. How has affliction in your life led to opportunities to comfort other saints?

Paul's hope for the saints in Corinth wasn't that they wouldn't suffer, but that—in their suffering—they would share in each other's comfort.

★ 4. What's the difference between passively waiting and "patiently endur[ing]"?

Review 1:8–10.

Many have offered possible explanations for the affliction Paul and his co-laborers experienced in Asia, including the riot in Ephesus (Acts 19:23–41) and an illness or other type of physical suffering.[3] Regardless of what the affliction was, it was so severe that it seems Paul genuinely expected to die at any moment. But because of that suffering, he wrote a comforting—both encouraging and instructive—reminder of the gospel.

5. Using 1:10 as your guide, match the time frame with the assurance of God's deliverance.

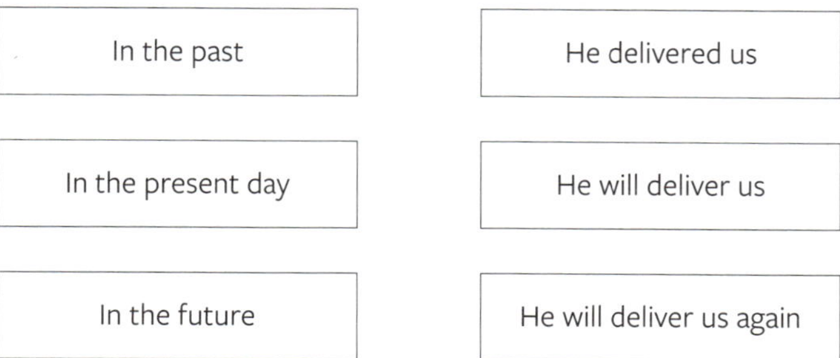

Review 1:11.

After reflecting on God's faithful deliverance from affliction in his life, Paul—undoubtedly anticipating more affliction—asked for prayer. If we truly believe that prayer is how we "bear one another's burdens" (Galatians 6:2), then by praying for a pastor or ministry leader, you join them in their work for the kingdom, making their burdens lighter and bringing them comfort in affliction.

6. Write a prayer for your pastor or a ministry leader below.

DAY 2

2 Corinthians 1:12–24

READ 2 CORINTHIANS 1:12–24

Like he had done before, Paul boasted. But he didn't boast about himself.

Review 1:12–14.

1. Complete the table below using 1:12.

	What is Paul's boast?
They behaved . . .	
Not by . . .	
But by . . .	
Toward . . .	

This boasting wasn't arrogance, but a humble confidence that rightly gave God the glory for all good things. In a powerful testimony to their reconciliation, Paul told the Corinthian church that just like they would undoubtedly boast about Paul and his co-laborers when Christ returns, Paul would also boast about *them*.

Review 1:15–16.

Paul spent the rest of this chapter recounting how his decisions about visiting them were indeed made with godly sincerity, despite changed plans.

2. On the map below, mark the paths of the following journeys.

Plan A (dotted line): Ephesus → Macedonia → Corinth (1 Corinthians 16:2–8)
Plan B (dashed line): Corinth → Macedonia → Corinth → Judea
Plan C (solid line): Ephesus → Corinth → Ephesus → Troas → Macedonia

Paul's plans had changed, which he didn't deny. But as a result, it seems that some of his opponents charged him with being untrustworthy. Based on how much he wrote about the topic in response, it's safe to assume that Paul was deeply troubled by these accusations.

★ 3. Why do you think accusations of untrustworthiness were so hurtful to Paul?

Review 1:17–19.

The world says *yes* when it means no, and it says no when it means yes. If Paul's plans had been of his own flesh, then he also would've been guilty of this. But Paul was led by God to postpone his visit to Corinth (which he would explain shortly). So that's what he did. And when he was accused of wrongdoing because he obeyed the Lord's leading, he basically said, *"Friends, I promise you I wasn't lying. As much as you're certain that God is good, you can be certain of this."*

In the midst of Paul's pain here at being wrongly accused, there is a sobering but beautiful reminder that God can use any hard thing for His glory. In defending his character, Paul wrote a testimony of God's faithfulness that has been cherished by Christians for thousands of years.

Review 1:20–22.

4. **Look up *amen* (1:20) in a Greek lexicon.** What did you learn?

God established Paul, creating him, calling him, and putting him in the places where he'd minister. God anointed Paul, setting him apart and making him holy. God sealed Paul, protecting him. And God gave Paul His Spirit as a guarantee—or a down payment—for what was still to come. Since the beginning and forever, God does the doing. Because God is the one who always keeps His promises, we can confirm all plans made in Him with a wholehearted "amen"—let it be so!

Review 1:23–24.

After establishing that his changed plans were a result of submitting to God's plan, Paul began wrapping up his defense. When Paul originally intended to take a trip to see the Corinthians, he'd anticipated a joyful and encouraging reunion. But as Paul received reports of their egregious and unrepentant sin, God led him to change his plans. Instead of delivering a severe—and deserved—rebuke in person, Paul sent them a letter.

★ 5. What did Paul want for the Corinthians, according to 1:24? How might an in-person visit have hindered that?

DAY 3

2 Corinthians 2:1–17

READ 2 CORINTHIANS 2:1–17

As Paul wrapped up his defense of his change of plans, let's review why he was compelled to defend himself at all.

1. Complete the chart below.

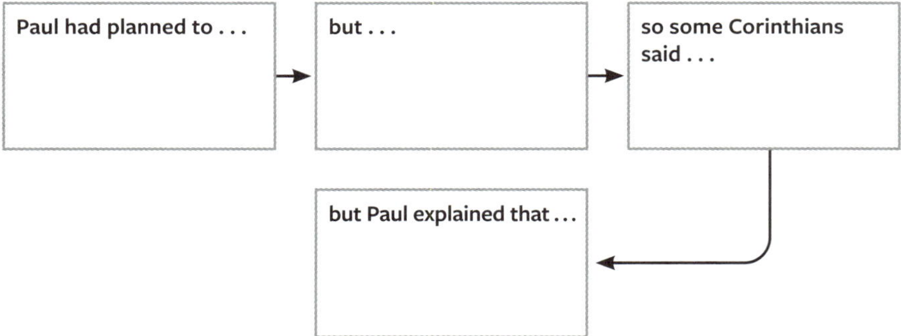

Review 2:1–4.

As he rested his case, Paul noted that another visit would've been painful for all of them. And while God certainly could have used a painful visit to accomplish His purposes, He chose to use a different tool: a letter. Some theologians think this letter was 1 Corinthians, while others think it was a letter that's since been lost[1]—we're calling it 1.5 Corinthians. Regardless of which letter it was, God used it to bring the Corinthians to repentance. Brokenhearted by their sin, Paul wrote with tears—not to shame them, but to show them love.

★ 2. Has the sin of someone you love broken your heart? What can Paul's example teach you?

With this freshly painted backdrop of love and repentance, Paul wrote to the Corinthians about their next right step: forgiveness.

Review 2:5–11.

A man from their church was in desperate need of forgiveness. This could have been the man from 1 Corinthians 5 who had an incestuous affair or the ringleader of the opposition against Paul and his ministry.[2] Whatever his sin was, it had impacted the entire church at Corinth.

As part of his discipline, the man had likely been excluded from the fellowship of the church. But by the time Paul wrote this letter, the man had repented; he should have been welcomed back. But his continued exclusion from the body was causing despair. Paul begged them to not just forgive and comfort him, but to reaffirm their love for him. Why? So that Satan and his schemes wouldn't win.

★ 3. What schemes of Satan could Paul have been referring to here? How are those still at play in our churches today?

Church discipline should be redemptive whenever possible, as Paul demonstrated. Our modern Christian culture can sometimes be quick to accuse and slow to restore—and both of those actions are steeped in arrogance. Christlike correction doesn't come from a desire to shame or cancel, but from a longing for redemption. May we never rebuke anyone with arrogance to tear them down, but only with abundant love to build up the body.

Review 2:12–17.

Paul changed topics to introduce one of the letter's main themes. But first, a short digression. This letter was written by Paul, after all.

4. What happened in Troas according to 2:12–13? Use a study Bible or commentary if you need help.

Remembering their joyful reunion in Macedonia, Paul painted a similar scene to the one he painted in 1 Corinthians 4: a victory parade.

5. Make a line drawing of a typical first-century Roman victory parade: a king and his general leading the victory march with captured prisoners of war and soldiers following behind, burning incense in celebration.

God is the king, victorious in battle, and Christ is the general, leading the victory march. Believers—once prisoners of our own sin—now joyfully march as soldiers with our King and General while spreading the aroma of the gospel.

The mention of this aroma would've reminded the Jewish believers in Paul's audience of Old Testament sacrifices (Leviticus 23:18; Numbers 28:27). This aroma came from sacrificed animal flesh but was *pleasing* to the Lord. Ever since Christ's sacrifice, this aroma has metaphorically come from His death and resurrection. To some, this aroma—or hearing the good news of the gospel—smells like death. (And make no mistake—this is a death they were already dying.) To others, it smells like life.

Death or life: a sobering reminder of what's at stake with the gospel. Believers aren't to be peddlers of a cheap and hollow message, but sincere proclaimers of the glorious and everlasting life made possible by Christ's death.

And with this mission in mind, Paul introduced a key theme of this letter.

6. What was Paul's rhetorical question from 2:16? What was the implied answer?

DAY 4

2 Corinthians 3:1–18

READ 2 CORINTHIANS 3:1–18

After reminding the Corinthians that they were proclaimers, not peddlers, Paul used that lens to address another issue in the early church: letters of recommendation. In the first century, traveling ministers would spend time moving from church to church. While some were legitimate, like Paul and his co-laborers, some weren't. The problem was that these false ministers were impressive—flashy, wealthy, and smooth—and they had letters of recommendation that proved their legitimacy (or so they claimed).[1]

Review 3:1–3.

While this issue might seem bound by a particular place and time, it can be closer to home than we'd like to admit. Today, a "letter of recommendation" might look like a degree from a particular institution, a social media endorsement by a particular leader, or a platform on a particular stage. Just like it was true then, it is true now: The minute we prioritize the image of those who minister to us is the minute we've lost sight of the one whose image we bear.

★ 1. What was Paul's letter of recommendation? Explain.

Paul had set up his theme of God's sufficiency a few sentences earlier, and here, he began to expand on it.

Review 3:4–6.

Paul's sufficiency for ministry was never actually Paul's. It was from God, through Christ, and by the Spirit. Paul explained that just like God called prophets in the Old Testament (Isaiah 6:1–8; Jeremiah 1:4–10; Ezekiel 1:1–3:11), He had called Paul to minister now (Acts 9:1–18). And the genuine change in the Corinthians' lives was proof of this! Paul's authority as an apostle was God-given. Paul's work as a servant and minister of the gospel was God-empowered. And this work—as a servant—was also the Corinthians' work, and also our work.

Around the same time that Paul wrote this letter, he wrote one to the believers in Rome; it's known to us as the book of Romans. In that letter he wrote, "Now we are released from the law, having died to that which held us captive, so that we serve in the new way of the Spirit and not in the old way of the written code" (Romans 7:6). Here, in 2 Corinthians 3, he taught further about the law, explaining the letter and the Spirit.

2. Match Paul's descriptions of the letter and the Spirit with their correct explanations.

The letter kills	The law explains God's standards without giving the power to keep them.
The Spirit gives life	Only God can change a heart, enabling obedience.

Review 3:7–11.

Paul never said the law was bad. In fact, in the same section of Romans where he taught about the law, he wrote, "I delight in the law of God" (Romans 7:22). But the law was given under the old covenant, so it has distinct differences from the Spirit, given to believers after Jesus ushered in the new covenant.

★ 3. Review how Paul compared the old covenant and the new covenant.

	Old Covenant	New Covenant
Ministry of	death (3:7) (3:9)	(3:6)
Engraved on	(3:7)	human hearts (3:3)
Gives	death (3:7)	(3:6)
Brings	(3:9)	righteousness (3:9)
Is	(3:7, 9–11)	far more exceedingly glorious (3:9–11)
Is	being brought to an end/fading (3:7)	(3:11)

Review 3:12–16.

When Moses came down from Mount Sinai with the tablets of the law, he covered his face with a veil (Exodus 34:29–35). You may have been taught that Moses needed a veil because the Israelites couldn't handle seeing the effects of God's glory. But Paul explained that the full reason was that the Israelites couldn't handle *seeing God's glory fade away*. All along, the old covenant was temporary. It was good, but it was going to fade away. And in its fading, it pointed forward to a lasting glory: Christ was always the eternal plan.

4. According to 3:16, when is the veil over someone's heart removed?

Review 3:17–18.

God sets believers free from what's fading away. In doing so, He frees us from sin, death, and condemnation. And He frees us *to* forgiveness, obedience, and life.

Believers—Paul, the Corinthians, and all believers for all time—are unveiled. And with unveiled faces, we get to *behold* the glory of the Lord. Beholding doesn't only mean looking at. It means studying and contemplating and fixing our eyes. And as we do that, we are being transformed more and more into His image. What we behold, we become.

5. With your unveiled face, behold God's glory. Write a prayer of praise.

DAY 5

2 Corinthians 4:1–18

 READ 2 CORINTHIANS 4:1–18

Paul began today's section like this: *"Because of all of this—because He unveiled us and because He freed us to obedience and because He entrusted us with sharing His gospel, we won't get discouraged and we won't give up."*

Review 4:1–5.

1. What had Paul renounced (4:2)? What was he proclaiming (4:5)?

Paul called Satan the "god of this world" here, but don't misunderstand this—though Satan is at work, he's on a leash. God is the one, true, almighty, everlasting God—of this world and of the whole universe. And even though some are blind to it, the light of the gospel isn't any less glorious.

Review 4:6.

2. Complete the image below using 4:6.

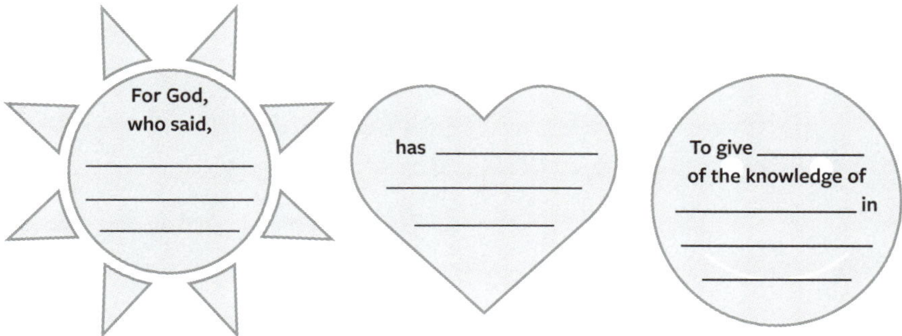

By going all the way back to creation, Paul drew another beautiful illustration. God brought light into darkness, both literally and figuratively. And when someone saw the light (or smelled the aroma of Christ) for the first time, they were unveiled. They beheld the glory of God in the face of Jesus.

Review 4:7.

3. What's the treasure Paul referred to in 4:7? (Use 4:1–6 for help if needed.)

A jar of clay was an easily understood metaphor in the first century. They were common vessels—imperfect and fragile—used to house all kinds of goods. But God chose these vessels to house *treasure*: Because of the gospel, the Spirit lives in believers. And with this priceless and eternal treasure living inside of him, Paul knew he could face anything.

Paul had already faced many trials, and he would face many more. But because "the surpassing power" (4:7) belonged to God all along, he could confidently say that his trials weren't the end for him.

Review 4:8–15.

4. What are some of the afflictions Paul faced? Why wasn't he destroyed by them?

Because of Jesus, Paul said his suffering didn't bring him death. And even more than that, he taught that his endurance through his suffering actually brought life—hope, encouragement, and instruction—to others in the early churches. And as those believers learned to endure through suffering because of Christ, more believers learned from them. As hope and trust increased from one believer to another, so did thanksgiving—so much that it abounded.

★ 5. Have you ever watched as a faithful believer endured through suffering? How did their example bring life to others? To you?

Review 4:16–18.

"So," Paul said, "*[because of this abounding hope, trust, grace, and thanksgiving]*, we do not lose heart." Paul had suffered, and he would suffer much more. At times, his suffering weighed so much that it was too heavy for him to bear (1:8). But he knew that God's glory weighed infinitely more. And compared to eternity? He said his suffering was light and momentary.

★ 6. How does Paul's understanding of suffering encourage you? How does it challenge you?

The reality for the believer is that we're already participating in the kingdom of God, but not yet living in the fully restored kingdom. We are imperfect, fragile vessels. And yet, we have the Spirit of God living in us. We are wasting away in death. And yet, we are inching forward toward eternal life. As we live our calling in a fallen, sinful world, we are—and will continue to be—afflicted. And yet, we have great hope.

We know that when Jesus returns, "He will wipe away every tear from their eyes, and death shall be no more, neither shall there be mourning, nor crying, nor pain anymore, for the former things have passed away" (Revelation 21:4). He will make all things new.

He's our light, He's our treasure, and He's where the joy is!

7. What stood out to you most in this week's study? Why?

8. What did you learn or relearn about God and His character this week?

DAY 6

Corresponding Psalm & Prayer

1. What correlation do you see between Psalm 30 and this week's study?

2. What portions of this psalm stand out to you most?

3. Close by praying this prayer aloud:

Father,

You are God our Father who sent our Lord Jesus Christ. You have brought me up and restored me to life. You comfort me in my affliction. You have delivered me, and You will deliver me again. You have removed the veil from my heart, and I behold Your glory!

But I have been derailed by affliction, using it as an excuse to look away from You. I have made much of myself and little of You. And like the Corinthian church, I have been too harsh with others who have sinned, quick to accuse and slow to restore. Forgive my arrogance.

Like Paul and his co-laborers, let me behave with godly sincerity, not by earthly wisdom but by Your grace. If I boast in anything, may it be You. When I am afflicted, remind me that You are making all things new. Turn my mourning to dancing and my tears to praise—give me joy in the morning.

Only You are sufficient for these things, and I surrender my life to You, Lord. Every moment of my day, each decision I make, I yield my will and way to Your perfect will and way.

I love You too. Amen.

DAY 7

Rest, Catch Up, or Dig Deeper

WEEKLY CHALLENGE

On Day 5, Paul compared believers to jars of clay: imperfect, fragile vessels that God chooses as a dwelling place for His Spirit. Make or draw a small jar of clay, and place it somewhere you'll see it often, like on your desk or dresser. Let its presence remind you of God's all-sufficient strength in your weakness.

WEEK 8

2 Corinthians 5–7

Scripture to Memorize

When I was a child, I spoke like a child, I thought like a child, I reasoned like a child. When I became a man, I gave up childish ways.

1 Corinthians 13:11

DAILY BIBLE READING

Day 1: 2 Corinthians 5:1–10
Day 2: 2 Corinthians 5:11–21
Day 3: 2 Corinthians 6:1–13
Day 4: 2 Corinthians 6:14–7:1
Day 5: 2 Corinthians 7:2–16
Day 6: Psalm 119:65–72
Day 7: Catch-Up Day

Corresponds to Day 339 of *The Bible Recap*.

WEEKLY CHALLENGE

See page 201 for more information.

DAY 1

2 Corinthians 5:1–10

READ 2 CORINTHIANS 5:1–10

Review 5:1–4.

Picking up where he left off in last week's study, Paul continued to contrast the earthly and the eternal—our present and future realities.

1. Which of the following do you think Paul meant when he said, "We know"?

   A. "We wish"

   B. "We probably can count on"

   C. "We are certain"

   D. "We've got our fingers crossed that"

Paul compared earthly bodies to tents when writing to these Corinthian believers, because it's a concept they were deeply familiar with. In this ancient culture, tents were often used as temporary homes for workers or travelers. Traveling groups might live in them for a season, the way the Israelites did in the desert when they were brought out of Egypt (Leviticus 23:42–43), or the way field workers did in Paul's time. In this agrarian society, workers erected tents, used them for a season, then tore them down and moved on to the next field. Tents were never meant to be long-term homes. They were—by nature, form, and function—temporary.

2. Using 5:1–3 as a guide, fill in the blank to complete Paul's following analogy.

> "A tent" refers to our earthly body, as "a building from God, a house" refers to our ______________ body.

Greek philosophers considered the human body a prison for the soul. They regarded a disembodied spirit as the ultimate state to be attained. But Paul was clear about what awaits us as believers on the other side of death. It's a real body, a perfect one. Resurrected believers will not be disembodied spirits—we will be *further* clothed (5:4), something we long and groan for.

Ecclesiastes 3:11 says God has set eternity in our hearts. And Romans 8:22–23 says, "The whole creation has been groaning together" along with us for "the redemption of our bodies." Creation groans with us for the splendor that awaits all God's kids. And when that time comes, what is mortal will be "swallowed up." There will be nothing of mortality left. That is a promise. This surely would've been an encouragement to the Corinthian church, as it is to us today.

Review 5:5–10.

God gave us the Holy Spirit as a guarantee of what He has waiting for all believers, like a down payment. But this isn't a modern-day type of down payment, with contingencies and fine print. *Arrabōn* is the Greek word used here; it means a payment that guarantees the recipient a legal claim.

For this reason, believers are always confident or "of good courage." While we are at home in our earthly bodies, we're away from the Lord, so Paul said, "We would rather be away from the body and at home with the Lord." It's something to look forward to!

★ 3. What do you think 5:8 means?

Because Paul was so confident of what awaited him after death, his response to the end of his earthly body was basically, "*Great! That's like taking down a tent you were going take down at some point anyway. It was always temporary. Taking down the tent just means I'm going to be with God forever.*"

Paul wasn't being glib about suffering and death. As we'll dig into more later in this week's study, he was deeply acquainted with the pain of bodily suffering and death. His point here was that these tents were never meant to be eternal, and what awaits us is so much better than what we've got. And when we *know* that, we're confident and of good courage even in the face of the destruction of our earthly tents.

★ 4. Does this kind of confidence feel unrealistic to you? Why or why not?

5. Write a prayer that God would bring you into fuller confidence in any places where this certainty is hard to grasp or imagine.

Despite common misconception, the judgment seat Paul referred to in 5:10 is not the judgment seat of salvation unbelievers will appear before (that is the great white throne judgment from Revelation 20:11–15). Salvation is *not* judged on a scale or deed by deed. Salvation comes through Christ alone.

The judgment seat Paul referred to here is the judgment seat that only believers will appear before—called the bema seat—where believers will be rewarded for their deeds. Eventually, our old bodies will be gone, but what will remain eternally will be whatever we did with those bodies while we were on earth. So, with good courage, let's use these old tents while we have them for the glory of God.

DAY 2

2 Corinthians 5:11–21

 READ 2 CORINTHIANS 5:11–21

Review 5:11–15.

The phrase "fear of the Lord" appears often in Scripture. And our modern use of the word *fear* is nothing like the scriptural meaning. The biblical definition of "fear of the Lord" consists primarily of delight and awe and denotes a reverence for the Lord's way and His mastery over all things. Paul was basically saying to the Corinthians, "*Therefore, having wisdom, and being aligned with God's way of doing things rather than man's, I will say everything else I'm about to say.*"

Paul didn't need to persuade God of what he was. And he was disappointed he needed to persuade the Corinthians of it. He said he'd hoped the Corinthians' consciences would also know him, but clearly many of them didn't, considering he had to write this portion of the letter.

People were looking down on Paul because he was suffering. Corinthian Christians thought the trials and sufferings Paul experienced made him less of a man of God, less of an apostle, not more of one. And Paul was disappointed that he had to remind them—"boast" of all they'd accomplished—so they'd be able to answer those who were judging them by man's standards.

Equating suffering with being less of an apostle instead of more of one is completely contrary to the gospel. But it happened to Paul with the Corinthian Christians, and it continues to happen today.

★ 1. There's something uniquely discouraging about having to defend your sufferings—especially if it's to people you didn't expect to have to defend yourself to. Have you experienced a situation similar to Paul's? Or have you ever found yourself falling into the kind of thinking some of the Corinthian Christians had fallen into?

How wounding it must have been for Paul to have to remind them of who he was before God, considering the reason they started doubting was because he was suffering *for* God—and for them. The phrase "beside ourselves" refers to being out of one's mind. The Corinthians thought Paul was insane for claiming to be content in his sufferings. (If you're curious about what all that suffering entailed, 2 Corinthians 11–12 goes into detail.) But whether he seemed sane or not, he did it all for God and in service to them.

2. In 5:14, what did Paul say controls us? Who do you think he meant by "us"?

Review 5:16–21.

Paul may have witnessed Jesus's teachings while Jesus was still alive. In His earthly ministry, Jesus was accused of being out of His mind and a menace to society. And Paul may have even been among the Pharisees who confronted Jesus. But by this point in Paul's life, he knew Christ through the Holy Spirit. Paul knew he would be a new creation, because he was once a persecutor of Jesus's followers. And Jesus had taken that persecution personally.

3. What did Jesus say to Paul (a.k.a. Saul) in Acts 9:4?

Jesus so closely identifies with the suffering of believers that He takes it personally. Jesus didn't ask Paul why he was persecuting *them*. He said, "Why are you persecuting me?"

4. Fill in the missing words from this paraphrase of Paul's statement in 5:17.

_________ can become a new creation in Christ. That is available to _______.

However, being a new creation doesn't mean we're perfect—it means we're changed and we're *being* changed, renewed day by day (2 Corinthians 4:16).

Reconciliation is a coming together or the repairing of a relationship. God reconciled Himself to us—that is, made a way for us to be with Him for all eternity—through Christ. Reconciliation happened through self-sacrifice, which is the model and message of reconciliation. That's how it happens. And so we are called to the same. Paul called not just the most well-known apostles but *all* believers "ambassadors for Christ."

Thankfully, Paul told the Corinthian Christians this call wasn't based on their own works, which was likely an invitation to boldness for them. Their boldness in serving as ambassadors for Christ was based on Christ's perfection, not their own. Some theologians refer to this concept as the Great Exchange, where Christ takes on our sin and grants us His righteousness. What an incredibly generous exchange!

★ 5. Is this good news to you? Have you ever been less bold in sharing your faith because of past sins? How does Christ's willingness to take on our sin that we "might become the righteousness of God" (5:21) encourage you into greater boldness?

DAY 3

2 Corinthians 6:1–13

READ 2 CORINTHIANS 6:1–13

Review 6:1–2.

Yesterday, Paul told the Corinthian Christians that they were ambassadors for Christ. Here, he explained that they were coworkers with Christ. The King of the universe invited them to be coworkers with Him! He didn't *need* them—but He *chose* them and invited them.

1. Does being a coworker with Christ impact your feelings about your job or roles in life? How so?

Grace is, by definition, a free gift. But how we steward that gift can determine how effective it is. Grace isn't given because of works, but it *is* given to encourage work with Him. We must not receive His grace in vain. In 6:2, Paul quoted Isaiah 49:8 to give the Corinthians a sense of urgency. Now is the time for this work.

Review 6:3–10.

Paul and his fellow apostles had gone out of their way to remove any stumbling blocks for the Corinthians. He had waived his salary (1 Corinthians 9:3–15), he had "become all things to all people" (1 Corinthians 9:19–23), and still, they brought criticism before him, pretending it was the reason for their heart posture. So Paul appealed to their Greek culture once again, laying evidence down logically, one item at a time.

In 2 Corinthians 6:4–5, Paul listed the many ways his personal liberties were put aside for the gospel—in the sufferings put upon him by others and even some he willingly chose. But in 6:6–7, he made sure to give credit where credit was due, listing the resources God graciously gave him to endure it.

2. What were those resources?

"Weapons of righteousness for the right hand and for the left" refers to wielding a spiritual sword in one hand and a shield in the other—both defensive and offensive weapons of protection and provision given to him by God.

In 6:8–10, Paul circled back to yesterday's study on the difference between how man sees situations and how God sees them. In these verses, Paul taps into something that shows up as a thread in this letter: the relationship between their sorrows and their ability to have joy. This kind of relationship requires a kingdom perspective; it's not of this world. (We'll see this affliction-joy connection again in 7:4 and 8:2.)

3. Using 6:8–10, fill out the status reports below. On the left side, list the world's descriptions of Paul. On the right side, list God's descriptions of Paul. The first one has been filled out for you.

How the world (and perhaps many of the Corinthian Christians) viewed Paul/his situation	How God viewed Paul/his situation
• dishonor (6:8)	• honor (6:8)

★ 4. Have you ever been in a situation—or are you in one now—in which the world saw you very differently from how God sees you? Fill out the status reports below. Let the way God sees you bring new strength, endurance, defiance in the face of discouragement, and confident expectation that He is working things for His glory into your situation.

How the world views me/my situation	How God views me/my situation

Review 6:11–13.

In today's final passage, Paul calls out a phenomenon that might feel familiar to modern readers. The Corinthians were pretending that Paul's instructions for godly living were inhibiting their ability to be in loving relationship with him. And he essentially said, "*Grow up and be honest.*" He said his love was completely open to them, completely unrestricted. But their love for lesser things was what restricted them from offering their love.

★ 5. "Widen your hearts" can be a challenging concept to consider. Are there ways that lesser loves have inhibited you from having a more loving relationship with God or with other believers? What do you think widening your heart would look like in those situations?

DAY 4

2 Corinthians 6:14–7:1

 **READ 2 CORINTHIANS 6:14–7:1**

Review 6:14–18.

Yesterday, Paul told the Corinthian Christians they were "restricted in [their] own affections" (6:12). Their love for lesser things was inhibiting their ability to live in a better, more worthwhile love. In keeping with the theme of being restricted by the wrong type of affections, Paul painted a picture they would've easily understood.

A yoke is a device that connects two animals to each other. The phrase "unequally yoked" is based on Deuteronomy 22:9–10, which instructed the Israelites not to yoke together two different kinds of animals to plow a field. A yoke helped the two animals share a load so that their combined strength could accomplish more work with greater efficiency. But if those two animals weren't equally matched, they would be restricted in their ability to work together and thrive.

1. The yoke on the left illustrates what equally yoked animals look like. In the yoke on the right, draw a mouse and elephant yoked together. Or a duck and rhinoceros. Or a giraffe and bunny. (Don't worry about how well you draw, because—spoiler alert—they're all going to be terribly matched anyway!)

★ 2. On a scale of 1–10, how confident would you be about your farm work getting done if you'd hired the mouse and elephant team for the job? Does this clarify any relationships where you've felt like you've been going in circles because you're moving at different paces?

★ 3. Does this compel you to make any adjustments in your relationships or in your expectations of those relationships?

A common misconception with this metaphor is that it applies exclusively to marriages. But the word *marriage* is nowhere in the verse. That's not to say that it doesn't apply to marriages—it does. But Paul was speaking to the Corinthian Christians about all their relationships. It requires us to widen our view of this verse to encompass even more areas.

4. Based on 1 Corinthians 5:9–13, 1 Corinthians 7:10–16, and yesterday's reading, put a check by the statements that are true.

- ☐ Paul told the Corinthian Christians to never associate with unbelievers.
- ☐ Paul told believers who were married to unbelievers to divorce them.
- ☐ Paul told the Corinthian Christians that they were being too indiscriminate in their loves and it was inhibiting their love for God and their capacity for godly loving relationships.

When Paul rhetorically asked what fellowship light has with darkness, or Christ with Belial, he assumed the answer was obvious. Belial is a Hebrew reference to something that is worthless or wicked, and sometimes it's a reference to Satan.

5. According to 6:16, who is the temple of the living God?

This is an astounding statement, and Paul referenced multiple Old Testament passages to make his point (including Isaiah 52:11 and Jeremiah 31:9). He told them to recall the incredible things God said about how *He Himself* would dwell among the Israelites in the temple they would build for Him. Paul reminded the New Testament believers, "*You are that temple of the living God.*"

Like God promised the Israelites in the Old Testament, the Corinthian Christians should also separate themselves from worthless stuff so that they could walk in unhindered fellowship with God—that they might be sons and daughters of the Lord Almighty!

6. **The Greek word used for *Almighty* in this passage (6:18), is *pantokratōr*.** Look up this word in a lexicon and write what you find below.

Review 7:1.

Moses's words in Exodus 20:18–21 help us understand the distinction between earthly fear, which draws us away from God, and the "fear of God" mentioned in 7:1, which draws us *to* God: "Do not fear . . . that the fear of him may be before you." There's an earthly fear that brings dread. But God tells us not to fear so that a *better fear*, a *good* fear, may be before us.

As we learned on Day 2, the "fear of the Lord" acknowledges His supremacy over everything that threatens to make us afraid. It's one of awe and delight—like experiencing the powerful roar of a mighty waterfall or seeing the vastness of the Grand Canyon. The fear of God might, ironically, look to earthly eyes like absolute fearlessness. It might look like Daniel sitting defiantly among lions (Daniel 6). It might look like Shadrach, Meshach, and Abednego in the furnace (Daniel 3). It might look like Esther saying, "If I perish, I perish" (Esther 4:16).

7. Describe a personal experience that helped you understand this good fear.

Remembering His promises will help connect us with the good fear that encourages our obedience. And our obedience moves us toward greater maturity in our relationship with God.

8. What do God's promises compel the Corinthians to do?

DAY 5

2 Corinthians 7:2–16

 READ 2 CORINTHIANS 7:2–16

Review 7:2–4.

Paul continues a theme today: rejoicing amid sorrow. We saw it in 6:10, and we'll see it again in 8:2. But here, Paul attributed his joy to something very specific: the Corinthian Christians' response to his letter (which we'll discuss more in a moment). He was bold in his correction, but here he was bold in his pride and joy for them. This is what we call a glowing report.

Review 7:5–11.

In Macedonia, Paul had many troubles—both outside conflicts and inside fears. And when he mentioned the coming of Titus, he was finally returning to a comment he made way back in 2:13. Basically, 2 Corinthians 2:14–7:4 is one long, Holy Spirit–inspired rabbit trail (which contains abundant treasures!). Let's look back at 2:13 to get our bearings.

1. In your own words, what does 2:13 say?

In 7:6–8, Paul said he was thrilled—not only because Titus had been safely returned to him, but also because of Titus's report about how the Corinthian Christians had received both Titus and the letter Paul had sent him to deliver.

This letter was "1.5 Corinthians," which we discussed in the introduction and earlier in our study. And in 7:8–9, Paul said *he* was grieved that the Corinthian Christians were grieved by the challenging and correcting content of his letter. But he didn't truly regret it, because the benefit of their response far outweighed the initial grief.

2. On the trees below, write what fruit each kind of grief produces (7:9–11).

Godly Grief

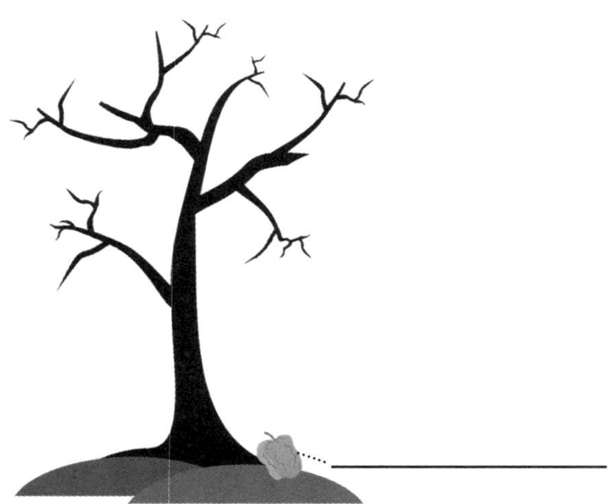

Worldly Grief

Two of Jesus's disciples serve as potent examples of these two types of grief: Peter and Judas. During Jesus's final day on earth before His crucifixion, these two disciples committed heinous sins against Him—denial and betrayal—and they both regretted it. Judas's regret (worldly grief) terminated on himself and ended in death (Matthew 27:3–10), but Peter's regret (godly grief) drove him deeper into repentance and resulted in forgiveness and a kingdom-centric assignment from Jesus: the call to feed His sheep (John 21:17).

3. Do you think the fear Paul referred to in 7:11 was a worldly fear or the fear of the Lord? (Recall yesterday's lesson about "good fear" in 7:1.)

The same idea applies to the word *punishment* (7:11). The original Greek is translated as "the avenging of wrong." This grieved state didn't lead to a hung head, but a vigorous passion—not a passive state, but a desire for action.

★ 4. Referencing 2 Corinthians 7:10–11, describe the difference between grief without God and grief with God.

★ 5. Describe a time in your life that highlighted the difference between worldly and godly grief.

Review 7:12–16.

Here, Paul addressed a past grievance among the Corinthians—but not for the sake of dragging up an old issue between them or taking sides. Paul addressed this in the letter to show how earnestly he loved them.

His words in 7:13–15 could imply that Titus was nervous to deliver Paul's letter. After all, the phrase "don't kill the messenger" hearkens to ancient cultures in which messengers who delivered unfavorable news were sometimes killed. And the Corinthian culture wasn't exactly tame. Titus may have been afraid or may have doubted they'd receive the letter with genuine hearts. In either case, Titus returned not just with glowing news about the Corinthians' reverent and obedient response to the letter but with a refreshed spirit. That's the beauty of God's correcting work. When it's done in love, all parties can come out on the other side refreshed and new. See what that godly sorrow produced!

Throughout 1 Corinthians, Paul spoke to them on their level with sarcastic turns of phrases such as, "Shall I commend you in this?" (1 Corinthians 11:22) and "You remember me in everything" (1 Corinthians 11:2). But in this letter, in 7:16, Paul rejoiced—no sarcasm needed. They'd received the corrections he made in love, and his boasts about them were not put to shame. They repented so genuinely that his confidence in them was complete.

This is the work God does in hearts. He brings about genuine change that blesses not just the person, but the whole! He's where the joy is!

6. What stood out to you most in this week's study? Why?

7. What did you learn or relearn about God and His character this week?

DAY 6

Corresponding Psalm & Prayer

READ PSALM 119:65–72

1. What correlation do you see between Psalm 119:65–72 and this week's study?

2. What portions of this psalm stand out to you most?

3. Close by praying this prayer aloud:

Father,

You created me and You're making me into a new creation. You've given me a good earthly tent that You bless now, and You'll give me an eternal home where I'll dwell with You forever. You've given Your Holy Spirit as a down payment, and my future is guaranteed. You are good and You do good—You have been so good to me, Your servant!

But I haven't been the servant I want to be. I've unequally yoked myself to those who don't believe in You—so I've walked in circles. I've tried to dim or downplay Your light—so I've walked in darkness. I've feared what the world thinks of me, but I haven't feared You. I've loved lesser things. I regret my sins and I repent of them.

Teach me good judgment and knowledge, because I believe Your commandments are best. Teach me to delight in You, to be in awe of You, to draw closer to You. May my holy fear of You make me fearless of this world.

I want to be Your joyful servant and Your faithful ambassador. I surrender my life to You, Lord—every moment of my day, each decision I make, I yield my will and way to Your perfect will and way.

I love You too. Amen.

DAY 7

Rest, Catch Up, or Dig Deeper

WEEKLY CHALLENGE

On Day 5, we learned about the difference between worldly sorrow and godly sorrow. "Whereas worldly grief produces death" (2 Corinthians 7:10), godly grief produces much valuable fruit.

Think back on a particular area of sin or regret in your life. In that space where Satan may want you to camp out in worldly grief, God offers you the opportunity to lean into freedom and fruit.

Write out a prayer asking God to help you reframe this area of your life—how you view it, how you live in response to it, and how you lean into His love, mercy, and tenderness toward you. He's creating good fruit in you even in the most challenging circumstances!

WEEK 9

2 Corinthians 8–10

Scripture to Memorize

For now we see in a mirror dimly, but then face to face. Now I know in part; then I shall know fully, even as I have been fully known.

1 Corinthians 13:12

DAILY BIBLE READING

Day 1: 2 Corinthians 8:1–15
Day 2: 2 Corinthians 8:16–24
Day 3: 2 Corinthians 9:1–5
Day 4: 2 Corinthians 9:6–15
Day 5: 2 Corinthians 10:1–18
Day 6: Psalm 46
Day 7: Catch-Up Day

Corresponds to Days 339 and 340 of *The Bible Recap*.

WEEKLY CHALLENGE

See page 226 for more information.

DAY 1

2 Corinthians 8:1–15

 READ 2 CORINTHIANS 8:1–15

This week's study addresses the Corinthian church's involvement in a financial collection for believers in Jerusalem who were facing extreme poverty. Paul's admonishment to the Corinthians was for them to participate joyfully and generously in this collection for others. He set before them two examples of the type of generosity he anticipated from them.

Review 8:1–5.

Example #1: The Churches of Macedonia

1. Fill in the blanks in 8:2 about these churches.

"... for in a ____________ test of affliction, their ________________

of _______ and their _____________ poverty have overflowed into a

___________ of __________________ on their part."

Everything about that sentence is countercultural—both then and now. These Macedonian believers were under severe persecution. They were in extreme poverty. It's likely that all of this was the result of their commitment to Jesus. And yet, they had joy and generosity. How? Because of God's grace.

This is not the first mention of joy in the face of affliction. Remember the affliction-joy connection in 6:10, where the apostles were "sorrowful, yet always rejoicing." And we saw it again in 7:4, where Paul said, "In all our affliction, I am overflowing with joy." Despite their continual afflictions, there was an abundance of joy. How is this possible? Again, God's grace.

★ 2. Why is it naturally hard to be joyful in difficult circumstances?

★ 3. Have you, or has someone you know, been "afflicted on every side" while still being carried along by an undercurrent of joy? Describe the experience.

4. Referencing 8:3–4, describe the Macedonian churches' level of giving.

Picture the scene. As Paul was ministering to the Macedonians, he was broken at the sight of their frail frames and tattered clothes, but he was also filled with joy as they smiled and shoved what little money they had into his hands for the sake of others. These were Christians who understood the words of 2 Samuel 24:24b, "I will not offer burnt offerings to the LORD my God that cost me nothing."

Once again, this was God's grace at work in their lives. This was victory through obedience. Their enemies could take their belongings, but no one could rob them of their joy in Christ.

Review 8:6–8.

5. List every way that Paul commended the Corinthians in 8:7. What was he referring to by "this act of grace"?

Paul had seen immense growth in the Corinthian church since his last letter. But giving to bless others would be an even greater sign of maturity. This is what would prove how genuine their love was.

Review 8:9–12.

If the sacrificial, joyful giving of the Macedonians didn't put enough of a fire in their bellies, Paul reminded them of the most gracious, sacrificial gift ever given.

Example #2: The Lord Jesus Christ

6. Fill in the blanks in 8:9.

> "For you know the __________ of our Lord Jesus Christ, that though he was rich, yet ______ ________ ________ he became poor . . ."

As we strive to look more like Christ, it starts here—by extending the same grace to others that we have received from Him. In this passage, grace is shown through generous giving. But God has called us to be gracious to all people, in all places, for all sorts of reasons, even sometimes when we don't want to.

God planted the desire in the Corinthians' hearts to give generously, and His Spirit would give them the follow-through. "For it is God who works in you, both to will and to work for his good pleasure" (Philippians 2:13).

7. Who is God calling you to be more gracious or generous toward? Ask God to let His grace flow through you as you are obedient in this area.

Review 8:13–15.

Because their giving was a product of God's grace in their lives, Paul assured them that this same grace would carry them and provide for them as they might have need in the future. This is an element of God's character that goes all the way back to the Israelites' beginnings. As they wandered in the desert, God provided actual food (manna) from heaven (Exodus 16). And drawing on this example in 8:15, Paul assured the Corinthians that as they gave obediently, they would have no lack. How? Because of grace.

DAY 2

2 Corinthians 8:16–24

READ 2 CORINTHIANS 8:16–24

1. Look back at 8:10. How much time had passed since the Corinthians first expressed a desire to take part in the offering?

It's possible Paul was addressing procrastination among the Corinthian Christians, but his exhortation was, as always, out of a desire to see them grow in Christlikeness.

Review 8:16–17.

Titus—one of Paul's companions during his stay in Corinth—appears to be the one who "encouraged [their] giving in the first place" (8:6 NLT), so he would return to them to help the Corinthians see it through.

2. Based on 8:16–17, how would you describe Titus's attitude toward the Corinthians? Why might this make him the perfect person to check in on their financial situation?

Twice here, the word *earnest* is used to describe Titus's ministry toward the Corinthians. The Greek word here is *spoudē* and means "haste, zeal, diligence, or enthusiasm." Titus did not go back to Corinth reluctantly. It would seem as though Paul's care for the church had rubbed off on him.

★ 3. Why might this visit have been uncomfortable? How did Titus's heart for the church soften the request?

We don't know how this request landed on the Corinthians; perhaps they were less money-sensitive than we are today. But even if it were challenging, Paul assured this congregation that his heart was in the right place. This wasn't about legalism or obligatory giving or anyone getting rich. Paul was calling on the Corinthians to fulfill the commitment *they* made a year ago. Like any good pastor, he was simply exhorting them toward continued growth and consistency in their walk with Christ.

Review 8:18–19.

Cue the theme song for *Unsolved Mysteries*! Much speculation has been made about who this unnamed "famous brother" was.

4. List everything you know about him from 8:18–19. (See an additional piece of info in 8:23b.)

Many scholars have speculated that this mystery brother could be Luke, Silas, Barnabas, or Timothy. But don't strain yourself trying to figure out who he was—in doing so, you'd miss the point. Though this brother might have been "famous" for his preaching, fame would have been counterintuitive for someone so committed to lifting up the name of Jesus. According to 8:19, he did all this work "for the glory of the Lord himself."

★ 5. Read John 3:30. In what ways does this statement go against human nature? How does it clash with our social media–driven culture today?

A second mystery brother is listed in 2 Corinthians 8:22. All we know about him is that he had been "tested and found earnest in many matters." And like the previous brother, he was also a "messenger," an apostle. Titus and his two mystery companions were not fundraisers, accountants, or slimy salesmen—they were men whose entire lives were gospel-centered, even in collecting an offering.

Review 8:20–24.

For some, being reminded to fulfill their pledge might feel uncomfortable, but Paul assured them their donations would be handled honorably.

6. Paul bragged on the generosity of the Corinthian believers to the churches in need. According to 8:24, what would their giving prove to these churches?

In essence, Paul said, "*You say you love the afflicted and poverty-stricken believers? Show me the money!*"

DAY 3

2 Corinthians 9:1–5

 READ 2 CORINTHIANS 9:1–5

Today's brief section of Paul's letter served as an important reminder to the Corinthian believers. He wanted to show them that it was not only the welfare of the impoverished believers that was at stake, but also their integrity as a church and his reputation as their representative.

Review 9:1–2.

Paul knew there was no need to educate the Corinthian church about the suffering believers in Jerusalem—they already knew their conditions and had committed to provide for them (9:2). This "ministry for the saints" would provide physical support, and it's safe to say it would be an emotional encouragement as well.

Today, we see this on social media in the world of crowdfunding. When someone goes through a tragedy or financial loss, even strangers will come together to provide funds for the person in need. The financial support for the individual is wonderful, but we're moved and encouraged as a society when we see this show of humanity in a dark world.

★ 1. Put yourself in the shoes of the suffering, impoverished believers in Jerusalem. What emotions would you have felt knowing that believers you hadn't even met were preparing a gift for you?

2. On the other hand, how might it affect you if they failed to keep that promise?

Before we assume anything negative about the Corinthians, it's important to note that we have no reason to think they failed to come through on their commitment. Paul just wasn't taking any chances. The church in Jerusalem was in a fragile state. And while even "the gates of hell shall not prevail against it" (Matthew 16:18), persecution, poverty, and dispersion abounded. There was no reason to add discouragement and division to the list of ills.

Review 9:3–4.

3. According to 9:3, why did Paul send Titus and the two mystery brothers to Corinth?

We learned in 1 Corinthians 16:1–4 that Paul had given Corinth specific instructions on how to prepare for this collection. A year ago, they'd been told to begin setting money aside every week—kind of like when your dad tells you to begin setting aside money for car insurance so you won't be blindsided when the annual invoice arrives.

Paul's words in 9:4 may sound a bit like a threat or ultimatum—almost as if he were saying, *"Don't make me come down there!"* But Paul knew a lot was at stake here. Not only before the Macedonians, but also before God.

Review 9:5.

If the brothers went to Corinth to assist in preparing the gift, this entire event could be much less stressful—it would be a joyful and willing gift. In fact, they would look more like the afflicted-but-joyful Macedonians.

4. **Look up the word for *exaction* in 9:5 in a Greek lexicon and write what you find. Then, look up *exaction* in an English dictionary and write the definition below.**

Paul knew that if the Corinthians weren't giving willingly, this wasn't a financial issue; it was a heart issue. He had seen how God's grace was enough for even the most impoverished people who gave obediently.

★ 5. Read Luke 21:1–4. Who caught Jesus's attention? Why do you think she gave so much?

As we seek to mirror the life of Christ, God is much more concerned with the posture of our hearts toward giving than *how much* we give. When we hold back what we think is rightfully ours instead of giving back to Him, it reveals a spirit of covetousness or greed. Giving joyfully and generously to others reflects the heart of our gracious Father toward us. And as we'll see tomorrow, it can even have a beautiful domino effect.

6. Do you find it difficult to give to the church (tithes/offerings)? Do you struggle to give to people in need? Write a prayer below asking God to give you a generous heart.

DAY 4

2 Corinthians 9:6–15

READ 2 CORINTHIANS 9:6–15

Today we'll conclude Paul's portion on giving (perhaps you're as relieved as the Corinthians!). Paul wrapped it up by pointing to the reasons for giving—because of the indescribable, undeserved gift all believers have received in Jesus.

Review 9:6–9.

Paul, once again appealing to this agrarian society, pointed to the principle of sowing and reaping. He wanted them to think logically about their giving. Just like the law of the harvest, they'd get out of it what they put into it. We see this again from Paul in Galatians 6, and Jesus taught His disciples a similar concept.

1. Read Luke 6:38 and describe Jesus's promise to those who give generously.

In 9:7, Paul reminded the Corinthians that this was a matter of the heart. Yesterday, we learned the term *exaction*—giving while expecting something in return. Yes, God will bless you as you bless others, but that is not why we give. God has shown us great mercy by sending Christ to save us. Anything else He gives us is a sheer act of grace. Of all people, Christians should be the most loving and the most generous. Our generosity is an overflow of our gratitude.

★ 2. Why do you think willing and joyful giving makes God so happy?

The Greek word for *cheerful*, used only here in the New Testament, is translated *hilaros*. Any guesses on what English word we get from this Greek term? Yes, our giving should be out of such happiness and overflowing gratitude that it feels hilarious!

3. According to 9:8, how does God's grace equip us for His work? Fill in the chart below.

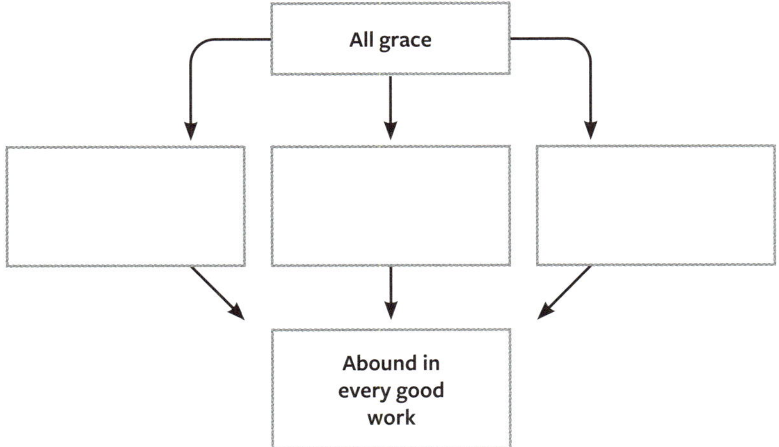

When our "readiness is there" (see 8:11–12), God provides everything we need to abound in good works for His glory.

At first glance we might assume 9:9 is talking about God. But when you read it in the context of Psalm 112, the "he" and "his" here actually refer to a righteous person. Those God has declared righteous distribute freely and give to the poor. This should be one of the marks of a Christ-follower.

Review 9:10–12.

4. Fill in the blanks in 9:10.

"He who supplies seed to the sower and bread for food will supply and multiply your seed for sowing and increase the harvest ______ ________ ________________________."

5. According to 9:11, why would God enrich the Corinthians in every way?

Giving isn't the path to personal prosperity and riches. It's the path to something far better: the opportunity to participate in God's work. When we're enriched in any way, God's desire is that we'd begin looking for ways to bless others, trusting that He'll continue to supply all our needs.

Review 9:13–15.

6. In 9:13, Paul said the saints would glorify God. What would they observe in the Corinthians that would cause this?

According to 9:14, this would not only impact the believers' relationship with God but also their relationships with each other. This is the fellowship of believers: that they would "long for you and pray for you, because of the surpassing grace of God upon you." Imagine it: people they've likely never even met so united in Christ that they long for each other and regularly intercede for one another.

It's no wonder Paul burst into an expression of praise as he closed this section.

★ 7. Write out 9:15. Below it, attempt to describe the indescribable gift of God's salvation.

DAY 5

2 Corinthians 10:1–18

READ 2 CORINTHIANS 10:1–18

There's a notable shift in Paul's tone in this portion of the letter. And while Paul did switch gears somewhat abruptly, he doubled down on the theme of the entire letter—exhorting the Corinthians to maturity and to walking in their Christ-given identity and power.

Review 10:1–2.

Paul used strong language in his appeal to the Corinthians. The point of his letter was to speak boldly to them and to be a louder voice than the false teachers who accused Paul of "walking according to the flesh."

1. Look back at 5:16–17. Why might this accusation carry such a personal charge for Paul?

Review 10:3–6.

You may be wondering, *Wait, why is Paul suddenly talking about warfare?* Because that's how seriously Paul took what was happening with respect to the false teachers and his Corinthian critics. They were accusing Paul of hypocrisy and trying to smear his reputation. By spreading lies about Paul, they were leading the Corinthian believers away from the truth and creating barriers—strongholds—that boxed out the truth of the gospel.

Paul's chief desire was to see the Corinthian church grow in their knowledge of and reliance on the gospel. And anything that sets itself up against the gospel must be demolished.

But Paul wasn't suggesting they declare physical war. Though they may be *of* the flesh (human), they would not wage war *through* the flesh. Paul would later expound on this in his letter to the Ephesians.

2. According to Ephesians 6:12, who are the true opponents of the gospel?

3. According to 2 Corinthians 10:4, what would it take to destroy these strongholds?

Paul's strategy for defending against the false teachers also had a broader application for the Corinthians—and for us. Using the divine power accessible to us because of our relationship with Jesus, we can "destroy every proud obstacle that keeps people from knowing God" (10:5 NLT). In fact, if you have experienced fear and discouragement about doing Bible studies like this one, recognize that those could be obstacles meant to keep you from knowing Christ and growing in your faith. But *every believer* has been given divine power to demolish those strongholds.

★ 4. **Using your favorite commentary, look up the phrase "take every thought captive" and write the meaning in your own words below.**

When we battle sin "according to the flesh," we succumb to the lie that we can outsmart our enemy, manage our sin, and white-knuckle our way through temptation. Instead, we could access the divine power that is available to us for tearing these strongholds down once and for all.

★ 5. Is there an area of sin, past or present, that Satan has made you think you can never overcome? How can this lie threaten your growth in Christlikeness?

6. Next to each verse below, list the ways believers are empowered to overcome sin.

1 Corinthians 2:5 ____________________

2 Peter 1:3 ____________________

2 Corinthians 6:7 ____________________

Romans 13:12 ____________________

Romans 12:2 ____________________

Above all, Paul wanted the Corinthians to remember their position in Christ and act accordingly—and by his God-given authority, he was prepared to punish anyone who threatened their freedom.

Review 10:7–12.

If they wanted to see divine power at work, they needed to look no further than Paul's ministry. Some have documented that he was not an impressive person in appearance, but it's more widely documented that Paul was one of the greatest preachers and disciple makers in history. He operated in the same divine power that he was calling the Corinthians to appropriate in their own lives.

7. Compare 10:8 and 13:10. What was Paul's reason for asserting his authority among the Corinthians? What was he *not* trying to do?

There was apparently a lot of chatter among the Corinthians about the nature of Paul's letters. He admitted his letters might be a bit strongly worded, but he had their spiritual maturity in mind. We may sometimes bristle at the guidance of a spiritual authority figure when it goes against what our flesh wants. But later we're thankful they were willing to give us truth when others might have let us go down the wrong path.

Review 10:13–18.

Paul's desire to spread the gospel had nothing to do with building up his own personal kingdom. As the Corinthians matured in their faith, naturally they would take the gospel to new places. In turn, Paul's sphere of influence would be enlarged. The Corinthians were disciples of Jesus who would become disciple makers. This would happen as God was glorified among them.

For the sake of the gospel, Paul defended himself to his critics, but he was unwilling to celebrate himself. As we've seen elsewhere, he would only boast in the Lord. Why seek approval, joy, or freedom from anyone else when He's where the joy is?

8. What stood out to you most in this week's study? Why?

9. What did you learn or relearn about God and His character this week?

DAY 6

Corresponding Psalm & Prayer

READ PSALM 46

1. What correlation do you see between Psalm 46 and this week's study?

2. What portions of this psalm stand out to you most?

3. Close by praying this prayer aloud:

Father,

You are my refuge and strength, my very present help in times of trouble. You sculpted the mountains, so I don't need to fear them moving. You poured out the seas, so I don't need to fear them rolling. You formed the earth, so I don't need to fear it crumbling. You are over all, and You are with me. You are mighty and You are near. You are the indescribable, undeserved gift!

I repent of my sins, Father. Even when I wasn't in danger of persecution, I've let fear lead. Even when I wasn't afflicted, I've let scarcity win. Even when You've blessed me, I've been downcast. Over and over, I have made myself increase, and I have made You decrease in importance in my heart.

Help me fear only You. Teach me to be generous. Equip me to be joyful. Train me to be earnest. Guide me to be still. Let me know You are God.

I surrender my life to You, Lord—every moment of my day, each decision I make, I yield my will and way to Your perfect will and way.

I love You too. Amen.

DAY 7

Rest, Catch Up, or Dig Deeper

WEEKLY CHALLENGE

On Day 1, we learned about the joy the Macedonians experienced as they gave to others in need, even though they were in poverty themselves. This week, no matter how little you have, there's room for generosity—even if it requires you to get creative!

Here are some starter ideas:

Purchase a gift card to a local grocery store or restaurant. Then ask your pastor or a leader in your church to give it to someone they know could use some help.

Offer to babysit, clean someone's home, or do some other act of kindness.

Ask God to show you an opportunity you might not think of otherwise.

WEEK 10

2 Corinthians 11–13

Scripture to Memorize

So now faith, hope, and love abide, these three; but the greatest of these is love.

1 Corinthians 13:13

DAILY BIBLE READING

Day 1: 2 Corinthians 11:1–15

Day 2: 2 Corinthians 11:16–33

Day 3: 2 Corinthians 12:1–10

Day 4: 2 Corinthians 12:11–21

Day 5: 2 Corinthians 13:1–14

Day 6: Psalm 91

Day 7: Catch-Up Day

Corresponds to Day 340 of *The Bible Recap*.

WEEKLY CHALLENGE

See page 250 for more information.

DAY 1

2 Corinthians 11:1–15

 READ 2 CORINTHIANS 11:1–15

Imagine watching a family member open an email from a scammer, clueless that it's a trap. Or looking over your teenager's shoulder as they interact with a social media account, and suddenly the "friend" behind the screen requests inappropriate photos. Wouldn't you cry out, "It's a scam! Stop! Look at the signs!"? That reaction is exactly what Paul expressed to the Corinthians in today's chapter.

Review 11:1–2.

1. **Using a dictionary, write the definition of the word *foolishness* below.**

Paul recognized that the Corinthians were being misled to believe his ministry to them was inferior. Though he shouldn't have had to defend it, he chose to use elements of Greek rhetoric to do so. But most importantly, he wanted them to know *truth*—not whatever the "super-apostles" were teaching. His godly jealousy targeted a desire for holiness in the church.

2. Based on our study, what are some of the sins this congregation was known for?

Paul used marriage imagery to reference the Jewish process of betrothal (engagement), where a woman was legally bound to her fiancé but remained a virgin for a year before the marriage ceremony. Despite the Corinthians' wicked history—even as saints—Paul was committed to their purity. How freeing and dignifying it must have been for them to hear themselves referred to as "pure virgins"!

Review 11:3–4.

Paul was incredibly concerned the Corinthians were being led away from truth, just as Satan had led Eve astray. Notice Paul wasn't concerned with defending his reputation. He was concerned about the church.

Greek culture valued strength over weakness, so it's likely these false apostles taught a "better Jesus" who didn't suffer like the real Jesus or call His followers to suffer. So 11:4 was Paul's way of saying, *"If you can listen to their absurd teaching, surely you'll let me make my case. And because I love you guys, I'm calling you out."*

Review 11:5–6.

3. What did Paul call himself in Ephesians 3:8?

"Super-apostles" was likely a nickname the false teachers had given themselves—and it wasn't a good one. The standards of Greek rhetoric expected teachers to speak with a polished, entertaining flair. Paul didn't have this training, but you can guess who did (and who some Corinthians wrongly listened to). Instead, Paul focused on clearly communicating the gospel, not merely attracting a crowd.

Review 11:7–10.

Sarcastic Paul showed up again, briefly, and he highlighted that, culturally, if a speaker didn't get paid for their teaching, they were regarded as lesser. Because Paul wasn't getting paid for leading the Corinthian church, some started questioning his apostleship. *Was he the real deal?*

★ 4. **Look up the Greek word for *robbed* (11:8) and write what you learn.**

Paul was a tentmaker (Acts 18:3). But as we've already learned, he quit making tents and relied on the financial support of the Macedonians. He never charged the Corinthians for his teaching. Unfortunately, some Corinthians were falling prey to the cultural appeal of the false teachers. They chose the teachings of the super-apostles, because those teachings came with the flashiest label and the highest price—but they were being scammed.

★ 5. Describe a time when you were tempted to listen to, buy, share, or spend time on something simply because it looked good on the outside, had a flashy name, or was expensive. Was it worth it? Explain.

Review 11:11–15.

Paul wanted to prove the super-apostles as frauds because he deeply loved the Corinthian Christians. While those teachers claimed to be just like him (and better), they weren't. No one can label or transform themself into an apostle—it's a calling from God.

Were these false teachers even believers? That wasn't the question. Paul's point was that these super-apostles looked more like Satan than Jesus. Just as Satan can disguise himself as an angel of light, people with bad intentions can "clean up nice." Calling themselves righteous didn't make the false teachers righteous. Only God could see what was going on in their hearts, and God would be the one to deal with them.

DAY 2

2 Corinthians 11:16–33

Review 11:16–21a.

While Paul would have much rather spent his words bragging on the worthiness of Jesus, he was forced to help the Corinthians understand why he was a legitimate apostle worth listening to.

1. Read Proverbs 26:5 and summarize it in your own words.

Likely with that proverb in mind, Paul talked about himself. His humility had been pushing the Corinthians away from his teaching. So once again, he turned to Greek rhetoric. (And this time, he paired sarcasm with some appropriate bragging.)

2. Look at 11:20. What did Paul suggest the false apostles were doing to the Corinthians?

The false apostles likely encouraged legalism and demanded the Corinthians be "slaves" to the Mosaic law (which Christ had fulfilled).[1] Remember, Greek audiences valued entertainment and confidence, so a prideful teaching style probably led to authoritarian leadership among the false apostles.

Some Corinthians were wooed by by their false teaching and bossy leadership, so they blindly obeyed. Paul called them out for irrationally putting up with inappropriate behaviors; however, the false teachers likely didn't actually slap them in the face—that was probably more sarcasm.

Review 11:21b–29.

While the false apostles claimed to be servants of Christ, their title didn't match their alleged "ministry." They should've been focusing on preaching the gospel where it hadn't been preached (Romans 15:20). Paul went on to speak "like a madman," because no super-apostle would ever brag about suffering endured while ministering to others.

If Paul had anything to brag about, it was his ancestry. But this isn't a valid Christian criterion for bragging; the only thing Christians should boast about is what God has done on the cross and in us.

3. Paul listed many of the dangers he faced while preaching the gospel. Match each danger and threat with its appropriate description. **You may need to use a commentary for research.**

Thirty-Nine Lashes	Historians agree: No one in the ancient world traveled by sea as much as Paul
Beaten with Rods	Concern for the churches felt like an oppressive weight he couldn't shake off
Stoned	Known for severe weather conditions
Shipwrecked	Likely an attempted execution or mob violence within a city
Rivers	It's likely Paul was mugged or at risk of being mugged while traveling between cities
Robbers	Crossings became dangerous if a rainstorm led to flooding
The Wilderness	When funds ran low, he couldn't cover his basic needs
False Brothers	Caused Paul grief from betrayal, disappointment, and extra work
Sleepless Nights	A Roman punishment citizens weren't supposed to experience
Hunger, Thirst, and Exposure	He taught or traveled twenty-four hours a day, seven days a week
Daily Pressure	From Deuteronomy 25:3, this Jewish punishment brought criminals close to death

Often, we think God supplying "every need" of ours means a life of ease or abundance—and at the least, the basics will be covered (Philippians 4:19). Yet for Paul, God's provision meant just enough to carry on, and it was uncomfortable. A hard life doesn't make you a Christian, but Paul freely chose this countercultural lifestyle out of his love for Jesus and the church.

★ 4. Describe a time when God's provision looked different from what you'd expected or hoped for.

When Paul called himself "weak," he was affirming the super-apostles' assessment. Yes, his life *was* marked by great weakness. However, Paul provided this list of weaknesses to demonstrate the lengths he was willing to go to for the churches he was leading. Of course Paul was angered by the false apostles' practices! They didn't care about the Corinthians like he did.

Review 11:30–33.

By highlighting weakness, Paul revealed God's sustaining grace. His suffering shifted the focus from personal pride to God's sufficiency. (Remember, the false apostles relied on self-sufficiency and the praise of men.) Paul knew God was honored by the honesty with which he shared, because only God knew his heart. But to communicate his point one more time, Paul gave another example.

5. **Using a commentary, do some research.** Why was Paul's escape via a basket another demonstration of humility and weakness?

★ 6. How did Jesus demonstrate humility? What might Paul have learned from Him? (See Philippians 2:5–8; John 5:19; Romans 5:7–11; John 8:28; John 13:4–5.)

DAY 3

2 Corinthians 12:1–10

READ 2 CORINTHIANS 12:1–10

Review 12:1.

Visions occurred frequently in the New Testament, but it's important to remember they were often (1) directed toward a specific individual, (2) subjective, and (3) prone to misunderstanding by readers today (Luke 1:8–23; Acts 7:55–56; Acts 12:9; Acts 22:6–11; Revelation 1:1).[1]

Review 12:2–6.

Paul used third person ("he") instead of first ("I"), but scholars agree he was talking about himself. Considering his style of communication in 11:16–33, it makes sense he'd still be talking about himself. This was the kind of spiritual event the super-apostles would've bragged about for days!

1. How many years had passed since Paul had the vision?

Make no mistake, Paul wasn't talking about alleged "levels of heaven." He used an antiquated way of thinking (though appropriate in his day): The first heaven was the sky—filled with birds and clouds, or even clear. The second heaven was what we call space—where the stars are. And in the vision, Paul thought he was in the "third heaven"—where God dwelled.

He compared it to a paradise—likely calling to mind a luxurious, royal Persian garden, according to Enduring Word's commentary. Some Christians reasonably believed this third heaven was where Christian souls went between death and resurrection.[2] Nonetheless, Paul was clear: If he didn't know exactly where he was, the Corinthians didn't need to know where he was.

2. Look at 12:3 and fill in the table below.

What did Paul know?	
What didn't Paul know?	
Who knew what Paul didn't know?	

Paul didn't dwell on what he saw or experienced. He only vaguely mentioned he'd heard something. Unlike others who might've used visions to promote themselves, Paul didn't seek to impress or claim special insight. Instead, he honestly and humbly shared, likely hoping the Corinthians would recognize that as a genuine apostle, he had authentic spiritual experiences.

He didn't camp out long talking about this scenario, though. Despite taking after the super-apostles' style of communication, he didn't *want* to boast about the vision. Paul had learned to value humility.

3. According to 12:6, why didn't Paul boast about the vision?

Review 12:7–8.

Whatever the contents of the vision were, they could have easily gone to Paul's head.

★ 4. What comfort do you find knowing the apostle Paul wasn't immune to the pitfalls of pride?

No one knows what the thorn was, but the Greek word suggests more of a tent stake than a thumbtack.[3] Scholars debate, but many have concluded it was blindness or poor vision (see Galatians 4:13, 15; 6:11). But whatever the thorn was, Paul said it was *given* to him.

How could Paul see the thorn as a gift if it was a "messenger of Satan"? As an educated Jew, Paul was undoubtedly well-acquainted with Job's story, when God allowed Satan's affliction. While God is never the active agent in evil, no hardship enters a believer's life without God's permission and His purpose for our good. Through Paul's experience, it's clear God cares greatly about humility. So in an encouraging twist, what Satan wanted to use to torment Paul, God used to sanctify him.

5. Paul practiced what he preached. Read Philippians 4:6. List any requests you need to bring to the Father.

6. Match each component of the thorn with its description.

The physical dimension	It was a messenger of Satan.
The spiritual dimension	God didn't give Paul the answer he wanted.
The emotional dimension	It was in his flesh.

Like Jesus in the garden of Gethsemane, Paul asked God to remove the thorn three times and God said no. While a no from God can be frustrating, it shouldn't necessarily be a surprise. Jesus told His followers they'd face trouble (John 16:33). So in the meantime, while awaiting ultimate relief from the brokenness of the world, believers like Paul (having been sealed with the Holy Spirit), are being strengthened and transformed (sanctified) to look more like Jesus (Revelation 21:4; 2 Corinthians 3:18).

Review 12:9–10.

★ 7. How would you respond if you prayed for something with the same three components as Paul's thorn and God's answer was "My grace is sufficient"? Are His grace and power really enough? Write your honest answer.

According to Paul, merely acknowledging Christ's sufficiency in our weakness has the effect of strengthening us. Oftentimes, Christians can't experience the power of Christ's sufficiency without first realizing how insufficient they are. As people physically grow up, they become increasingly independent. On the other hand, when people grow up in Christ, they become increasingly *dependent* on Him.

Today's reading concluded with Paul's picture of Christian maturity: When you are weak, then you are strong.

DAY 4

2 Corinthians 12:11–21

Review 12:11–13.

If talking about themselves worked for the super-apostles, Paul (motivated by love) was willing to beat them at their own game—but he hated it. Nevertheless, Paul proved he was a true apostle by pointing out that in addition to his title of apostle, God's power was at work within him.

1. Referencing 12:12, list the three examples of God's power at work in Paul.

He'd used sarcasm and bragging to correct the Corinthians' thinking; and now, in 12:13, he took another lesson from Greek rhetoric and turned to irony. It's likely Paul was responding to a claim that he played favorites with the churches (the Corinthians thinking they were his least favorite). Paul corrected their logic by pointing out they were claiming his refusal to charge them was sin when it was actually an act of grace.

Review 12:14–16.

Paul acknowledged he founded the Corinthian church, and much like a parent takes care of their children, he'd continue to care for them, expecting nothing in return. By doing so, Paul reflected the heart of Jesus—Jesus didn't die because of what He could get from sinners. He died and defeated death because He loved them (John 3:16).

Notice that Paul didn't hold a grudge against the Corinthians for not showing the same kind of Christlike love in return. In 12:16, it's clear the Corinthians had previously claimed Paul took advantage of them. This was likely because the super-apostles despised Paul's refusal to accept payment for his teaching and assigned a deceitful motive to undermine his generosity.

2. Fill in the blanks in 12:15a.

"I will most ____________ __________ and be __________ for your souls."

While Paul was addressing a specific cultural context, there's a principle for today: Christian leaders should never be motivated by what they can get from those they're leading. Rather, they should be motivated by what they can give—namely, the truth and love of Jesus.

Paul highlighted the inappropriate *motives* of the super-apostles: to get paid and make a name for themselves. Today, this doesn't mean Christian leaders shouldn't be compensated for their work or have large followings (1 Timothy 5:18). Paul was addressing the *intentions* behind leaders' actions, which stemmed from their hearts. If there are Christian leaders you know personally, and you're unsure whether they're trustworthy, consider whether their lifestyle generally reflects (or attempts to reflect) the heart of Jesus. (This is more difficult to accomplish if you don't know them personally.)

★ 3. Who is a Christian leader in your life who seems to reflect Christ's character? How do you know? Send them a message thanking them for their example.

Review 12:17–18.

Paul never behaved in a financially inappropriate way toward the Corinthians. Even when he sent Titus and the brother to the Corinthians, they'd all acted consistently with the character of Jesus.

Review 12:19–21.

4. In your own words, what question did Paul ask the Corinthians in 12:19?

Some scholars believe Paul's main goal was to defend his apostleship, while others think it was to express concern for the Corinthians. While Paul was using elements of Greek rhetoric, resembling someone on trial for a crime, he clarified his aim—everything Paul had said and done was intended to help the Corinthians grow in Christ.

Paul wrote that if he found the Corinthians stuck in the same old sinful habits on his third in-person visit, he'd be humbled and he'd mourn. Any change that could have occurred in the Corinthians wouldn't be because of Paul's efforts, thus the humility. It would have been due to the Holy Spirit's work in their hearts. If the Corinthians didn't surrender to the Spirit and change, Paul would be heartbroken over their decision to keep sinning. But make no mistake, just like Jesus, Paul wasn't looking for perfection; he was only hoping for repentance.

★ 5. Describe a time when you incorrectly thought that if you weren't perfect, you weren't a "good Christian." What helped you recognize the truth? (Bonus points if you use Scripture in your answer!)

DAY 5

2 Corinthians 13:1–14

READ 2 CORINTHIANS 13:1–14

Review 13:1–4.

In 2 Corinthians 12:14, Paul labeled himself the Corinthians' father. Here, he doubled down, seeking to care for the Corinthians as any compassionate dad would. He wanted to hold them accountable through discipleship, and if needed, discipline.

Paul reminded the Corinthians he'd lovingly called them to change their ways multiple times. His upcoming in-person evaluation shouldn't have been a surprise. But more than just correcting their behavior, Paul deeply cared about the state of their hearts—he wanted them to repent.

The Corinthians had sought proof of God's power in Paul, so as their reliable father figure, he made it clear they'd witness that power firsthand if they hadn't repented by the time he arrived in Corinth. It was like a dad saying, "Don't make me pull this car over."

Review 13:5.

There's a difference between cognitively knowing Jesus (knowing *about* Jesus) and knowing Him through faith (believing in Jesus *and* faithfully following Him out of gratitude for what He's done). While Paul spoke to the Corinthians as believers throughout both letters, he presented an opportunity for the Corinthians to "test" themselves.

The important thing to remember about tests is that you can't circle two answers—you either know the right answer or you don't. There's no in-between. And this wasn't a trick; Paul was providing a true or false question for the Corinthians.

1. Look back at 1 Corinthians 1:2 and 2 Corinthians 1:1. How did Paul describe the recipients of his letter?

2. As a reminder, and in light of those words, what issues in the church did Paul address throughout both letters?

After receiving letters chock-full of admonishment, the Corinthians may have been doubting their salvation. Perhaps Paul called the Corinthians to test themselves because he wanted them to be reminded that—despite all their sins and mistakes—their salvation was secure in Christ.

However, it's also possible Paul posed this question because the Corinthians' lifestyle wasn't matching up with the Christian identity they claimed; Paul could have been summing up his thoughts by calling them out. In John 14:15, Jesus said that if you love Him, you'll keep His commandments—and the Corinthians weren't. But solely following Jesus's commands (or just doing the right thing by being a "good person"—whatever that means) doesn't save you either.

Their answer on the test could have led them to Christ in a salvific sense or it could've led them to repentance in a sanctifying sense. And either way, Paul was doing his job. He was leading them to Jesus.

3. If you're applying Paul's test to your own life and feel unsure about your salvation, you're using the wrong test. A good test, paired with good study, allows you to circle the right answer confidently. To strengthen your answer on Paul's test, match the following verses to their contents.

Let's Study for the Test!

	There is no condemnation.
Romans 3:23	Faith necessitates faithful works.
Romans 10:9–10	Believers can find healing from sin through confession and prayer.
John 6:29	All people fall short of God's standard.
Ephesians 2:8–10	How to become a Christian
James 2:14, 17	When you believe in Christ, you are sealed with the Spirit. Your inheritance is guaranteed.
Romans 8:1	
Ephesians 1:13	Believers are saved by faith, not their works. No one can boast in their works.
1 John 5:11–13	The work of God in the sinner is through belief.
James 5:16	A reminder that if you believe in Christ, you are saved

★ 4. Now that you've studied, how would you answer Paul's test? How do you know?

Review 13:6–10.

After encouraging the Corinthians to test themselves, Paul acknowledged they'd been testing him and Timothy. Interestingly, Paul pointed out that the Corinthians were likely using the wrong test. The super-apostles would've taught the Corinthians to value power and financial gain. If that was what they were testing, Paul and Timothy certainly failed.

But once again, Paul embraced his role as loving father and reminded the Corinthians that his motivation was their restoration.

5. **Using a dictionary, define *restoration* (13:9).**

Review 13:11–14.

Paul referred to the Corinthians as his brothers in Christ and concluded his letter by encouraging them to get along. Remember all the people you've read about in this study—the idol-meat eaters and the meat avoiders, the rich and the poor, the repentant adulterers? They're the people Paul was encouraging to greet each other with a holy kiss. Much like a handshake today, the holy kiss was a sign of unity among believers of different backgrounds, races, genders, and convictions.[1] Paul called the Corinthians to an act of platonic physical affection that would have marked repentant and reconciled hearts. The entire body of believers was cheering them on.

Just as the Trinity is a picture of the unity found within the Godhead (Deuteronomy 6:4), Paul concluded his letter by mentioning all three persons: the love of the Father, the grace of the Son, and the fellowship of the Holy Spirit. What Paul wanted the Corinthians to achieve could never be done in their own strength, and he knew it! It was only by God's work that they could be transformed to walk in greater freedom and unity and to demonstrate Christ to the world around them. And what a beautiful transformation. He's where the joy is!

6. What stood out to you most in this week's study? Why?

★ 7. What did you learn or relearn about God and His character this week?

DAY 6

Corresponding Psalm & Prayer

READ PSALM 91

1. What correlation do you see between Psalm 91 and this week's study?

2. What portions of this psalm stand out to you most?

3. Close by praying this prayer aloud:

Father,

You built Your church and You've sustained it for thousands of years. No matter what happens around us, You're the place where we find refuge, safety, and peace. You command angel armies and You crush poisonous snakes. You're our dwelling place, solid foundation, and Savior. You hold us in love.

The Corinthians were marked by their sins, and so are we. We're also guilty of sexual immorality—adultery. We're also guilty of litigious pursuits—bitterness. We're also guilty of disorderly worship—pride. And we're also guilty of licentious indulgences—arrogance. I am guilty of adultery, bitterness, pride, and arrogance. I am less than the least of all of Your people, and I repent.

Thank You for Your abundant love for me and for Your forgiveness. I bring my requests to You. I ask You to provide, Lord. And Your provision might look different from what I'd hoped for, so please point my heart toward gratitude. Whether You answer yes or no, let me learn from Your example—let me be humble. Let me remember that the commander of armies is for me. Let me remember that the crusher of snakes is with me.

Whether You grant blessings or allow thorns, I accept them all as gifts—for Your glory and for my good. And so I surrender my life to You, Lord—every moment of my day, each decision I make, I yield my will and way to Your perfect will and way.

I love You too. Amen.

DAY 7

Rest, Catch Up, or Dig Deeper

WEEKLY CHALLENGE

As we conclude our study of 1 and 2 Corinthians, take some time to meditate on all you've learned. Flip back through and review your answers to the last question of each week's study, "What did you learn or relearn about God and His character?" Spend some time reflecting and journal a prayer thanking God for growing your understanding of Him.

FOR GROUP LEADERS

Thank you for using this study and leading others through it as well! Each week has a wide variety of content (daily Bible reading, content and questions, Scripture memorization, weekly challenge, and resources) to help the reader develop a range of spiritual disciplines. Feel free to include as much or as little of that in your meetings as you'd like. The details provided in How to Use This Study (pp. 9–11) will be helpful to you and all your group members, so be sure to review that information together!

It's up to you and your group how you'd like to structure your meetings, but we suggest including time for discussion of the week's study and Bible text, mutual encouragement, and prayer. You may also want to practice your Scripture memory verses together as a group or in pairs. As you share with each other, "consider how to stir up one another to love and good works" (Hebrews 10:24) and "encourage one another and build one another up" (1 Thessalonians 5:11).

Here are some sample questions to help facilitate discussion. This is structured as a weekly study, but if your group meets at a different frequency, you may wish to adjust the questions accordingly. Cover as many questions as time allows, or feel free to come up with your own. And don't forget to check out the additional resources we've linked for you at MyDGroup.org/Resources/Corinthians.

Sample Discussion Questions

What questions did this week's study or Bible text bring up for you?

What stood out to you in this week's study?

What did you notice about God and His character?

How were you challenged by your study of the Bible text? Is there anything you want to change in light of what you learned?

How does what you learned about God affect the way you live in community?

What correlation did you see between the psalm from Day 6 and this week's study of 1 Corinthians (or 2 Corinthians)?

Have you felt God working in you through the weekly challenge? If so, how?

Is your love for God's Word increasing as we go through this study? If so, how?

Did anything you learned increase your joy in knowing Jesus?

ACKNOWLEDGMENTS

Laura Buchelt, Emily Pickell, Abby Dane, Kirsten McCloskey, Emma Dotter, and Liz Suggs—thank you for your incredible research, creativity, wisdom, humility, and laughter. It's truly a blast to study God's Word with you all!

Sarah Billings—thank you for your skills of house-momming, chipmunk charming, and late-night chatting. And for teaching me the value of a griddle.

Lisa Jackson—you continue to be such a gift as a guide, agent, and friend.

And to the rest of the incredible D-Group Team—Rachel Mantooth, Lindsay Ruhter, Jane Long, Warwick Fuller, Meg Mitchell, Evaline Asmah, and our board, leaders, members, and church partners around the world—I love being on mission with you!

NOTES

Week 1: Day 2

1. "G2842 - koinōnia - Strong's Greek Lexicon (esv)," Blue Letter Bible, accessed 18 December, 2024, https://www.blueletterbible.org/lexicon/g2842/esv/mgnt/0-1/.

2. "1 Corinthians 1 – Jesus, the Wisdom of God," Enduring Word, https://enduringword.com/bible-commentary/1-corinthians-1/.

Week 3: Day 1

1. "1 Corinthians 7 – Principles Regarding Marriage and Singleness," Enduring Word, https://enduringword.com/bible-commentary/1-corinthians-7.

2. *The ESV Women's Study Bible* (Crossway, 2020), 1870n7:15.

Week 3: Day 2

1. Tremper Longman III and David E. Garland, eds., *The Expositor's Bible Commentary: Romans–Galatians*, rev. ed. (Zondervan Academic, 2008), 322n18.

Week 3: Day 3

1. Tremper Longman III and David E. Garland, eds., *The Expositor's Bible Commentary: Romans–Galatians*, rev. ed. (Zondervan Academic, 2008), 324n25.

2. *The ESV Women's Study Bible* (Crossway, 2020), 1872n7:26.

3. "1 Corinthians 7 – Principles Regarding Marriage and Singleness," Enduring Word, https://enduringword.com/bible-commentary/1-corinthians-7/.

Week 3: Day 4

1. Tremper Longman III and David E. Garland, eds., *The Expositor's Bible Commentary: Romans–Galatians*, rev. ed. (Zondervan Academic, 2008), 329.

2. "1 Corinthians 8 – Living by Knowledge or by Love," Enduring Word, https://enduringword.com/bible-commentary/1-corinthians-8/

Week 3: Day 5

1. Tremper Longman III and David E. Garland, eds., *The Expositor's Bible Commentary: Romans–Galatians*, rev. ed. (Zondervan Academic, 2008), 250.

2. *The ESV Women's Study Bible* (Crossway, 2020), 1875n9:24–27.

Week 5: Day 5

1. Manfred T. Brauch, *Hard Sayings of Paul* (InterVarsity Press, 1989), 170.

2. Leon Morris, *1 Corinthians: An Introduction and Commentary*, vol. 7 (InterVarsity Press, 1985), 192–194.

3. "1 Corinthians 14 – Tongues, Prophecy and Public Worship,: Enduring Word, https://enduringword.com/bible-commentary/1-corinthians-14/.

Week 6: Day 1

1. Justin Taylor, "Who Were the Six Women Who Saw the Risen Christ?" The Gospel Coalition, April 10, 2020, https://www.thegospelcoalition.org/blogs/justin-taylor/who-were-the-six-women-who-saw-the-risen-christ/.

Week 6: Day 2

1. Dr. Thomas L. Constable, *Notes on 1 Corinthians* (Sonic Light, 2024), p. 300, https://soniclight.com/tcon/notes/pdf/1corinthians.pdf.

2. "1 Corinthians 15 – The Resurrection of Jesus and Our Resurrection," Enduring Word, https://enduringword.com/bible-commentary/1-corinthians-15/.

Week 6: Day 3

1. Dr. Thomas L. Constable, *Notes on 1 Corinthians* (Sonic Light, 2024), p. 310–311, https://soniclight.com/tcon/notes/pdf/1corinthians.pdf.

Week 6: Day 4

1. "1 Corinthians 16 – A Collection and a Conclusion," Enduring Word, https://enduringword.com/bible-commentary/1-corinthians-16/.

Week 6: Day 5

1. Dr. Thomas L. Constable, *Notes on 1 Corinthians* (Sonic Light, 2024), p. 336, https://soniclight.com/tcon/notes/pdf/1corinthians.pdf.

Week 7: Day 1

1. Tremper Longman III and David E. Garland, eds., *The Expositor's Bible Commentary: Romans–Galatians*, rev. ed. (Zondervan Academic, 2008), 439–440.

2. *The ESV Women's Study Bible* (Crossway, 2020), 1895n1:3.

3. *The ESV Women's Study Bible* (Crossway, 2020), 1895n1:8; Tremper Longman III and David E. Garland, eds., *The Expositor's Bible Commentary: Romans–Galatians*, rev. ed. (Zondervan Academic, 2008), 443; "2 Corinthians 1 – The God of All Comfort," Enduring Word, https://enduringword.com/bible-commentary/2-corinthians-1/.

Week 7: Day 3

1. "2 Corinthians 2 – The Strategy of Satan and the Victory of Jesus," Enduring Word, https://enduringword.com/bible-commentary/2-corinthians-2/.

2. "2 Corinthians 2 – The Strategy of Satan and the Victory of Jesus," Enduring Word, https://enduringword.com/bible-commentary/2-corinthians-2/; *The ESV Women's Study Bible* (Crossway, 2020), 1897n2:5–11.

Week 7: Day 4

1. Tremper Longman III and David E. Garland, eds., *The Expositor's Bible Commentary: Romans–Galatians*, rev. ed. (Zondervan Academic, 2008), 458; Bethany L. Jenkins, "Letters of Recommendation," in *The ESV Women's Study Bible* (Crossway, 2020), 1900.

Week 10: Day 2

1. "2 Corinthians 11 – Paul's 'Foolish Boasting,'" Enduring Word, https://enduringword.com/bible-commentary/2-corinthians-11/.

Week 10: Day 3

1. "2 Corinthians 12 – The Strength of Grace in Weakness," Enduring Word, https://enduringword.com/bible-commentary/2-corinthians-12/.

2. "2 Corinthians 12 – The Strength of Grace in Weakness," Enduring Word, https://enduringword.com/bible-commentary/2-corinthians-12/.

3. "2 Corinthians 12 – The Strength of Grace in Weakness," Enduring Word, https://enduringword.com/bible-commentary/2-corinthians-12/.

Week 10: Day 5

1. "What Exactly Is a Holy Kiss?" Got Questions, https://www.gotquestions.org/holy-kiss.html.

ABOUT THE EDITOR

TARA-LEIGH COBBLE'S zeal for biblical literacy is at the heart of everything she creates. Her goal is to help people read, understand, and love the Bible. Her daily podcast, *The Bible Recap*, guides listeners through a chronological one-year reading plan. The podcast has over 400 million downloads and reached number one on the Apple Podcast charts in All Categories. She created and leads D-Group International, which has grown into an international network of nearly 400 weekly Bible studies that meet in homes, in churches, and online. A *Wall Street Journal* bestselling author, she also writes and hosts a daily radio feature called *The God Shot*, and leads trips to Israel to study the Bible on-site. Tara-Leigh lives in Dallas, Texas, where she has no pets, children, or anything else that might die if she forgets to feed it.

For more information: TaraLeighCobble.com | TheBibleRecap.com | MyDGroup.org | Israelux.com
Social media: @taraleighcobble | @thebiblerecap | @mydgroup | @israeluxtours

MINISTRIES

THE BIBLE RECAP—*READ THE BIBLE*

Est. 2019 | TheBibleRecap.com
Have you ever closed your Bible and thought, *What did I just read?* In about eight minutes a day, our summary walks you through the one-year chronological plan. Available in podcast, YouTube, and book form. Other supplemental resources available for adults and children.

D-GROUP INTERNATIONAL—*STUDY THE BIBLE*

Est. 2009 | MyDGroup.org
Men's and women's Bible study groups that meet weekly—in homes, online, and in churches around the world. D-Group recently began a series of 40 studies that will cover the entire Bible over the course of a decade.

ISRAELUX—*EXPERIENCE THE BIBLE*

Est. 2014 | Israelux.com
Offering a deluxe tour, incredible dining experiences, luxury accommodations, and life-changing teaching at biblical sites. The beauty of Israel is also captured in TLC's book *Israel: Beauty, Light, and Luxury,* a *Wall Street Journal* bestseller.